M000112756

WE ARE A MASTERPIECE

By **Gina Femia**

STEELE SPRING
STAGE RIGHTS

www.stagerights.com

WE ARE A MASTERPIECE
Copyright © 2018 by Gina Femia
All Rights Reserved

All performances and public readings of WE ARE A MASTERPIECE are subject to royalties. It is fully protected under the copyright laws of the United States of America, of all countries covered by the International Copyright Union, of all countries covered by the Pan-American Copyright Convention and the Universal Copyright Convention, and all countries with which the United States has reciprocal copyright relations. All rights are strictly reserved.

No part of this book may be reproduced, stored in a retrieval system, or transmitted in any form, by any means, including mechanical, electronic, photocopying, recording, or otherwise, without the prior written permission of the author. Publication of this play does not necessarily imply that it is available for performance by amateurs or professionals. It is strongly recommended all interested parties apply to Steele Spring Stage Rights for performance rights before starting rehearsals or advertising.

No changes shall be made in the play for the purpose of your production without prior written consent. All billing stipulations in your license agreement must be strictly adhered to. No person, firm or entity may receive credit larger or more prominent than that accorded the Author.

For all stage performance inquiries, please contact:

Steele Spring Stage Rights
3845 Cazador Street
Los Angeles, CA 90065
(323) 739-0413
www.stagerights.com

PRODUCTION HISTORY

We Are a Masterpiece was commissioned and developed through Retro Productions Theatre Company and received its world premiere in a co-production between Retro and the 14th Street Y Theatre in New York City with support from the Arch and Bruce Foundation.

We Are a Masterpiece was originally produced by Retro Productions Theater Company (Heather Cuningham, Producing Artistic Director) in New York City in April 2018. It was directed by DeLisa White; the set design was by Rebecca and Jack Cunningham; the costume design was by Viviane Galloway; the lighting design was by Asa Lipton; the sound design was by Jacob Subotnick; the properties were designed by Sara Slagle; the dramaturg was Molly Marinek, and the production stage manager was Elizabeth Ramsey. The cast was as follows:

Heather E. Cunningham, Pilar Gonzalez, Sam Heldt, Chad Miller, Ben Schnickel, Ric Seacrest, Sara Thigpen, and Matthew Trumbull.

Photos by Rick Sechrest.

WE ARE A MASTERPIECE

FOLKS

Minimum Casting Requirement: 3F, 5M

JOAN: Our protagonist. A really great nurse. Hard but has a giant heart, 40s, female.

RYAN MILLER: Older, an art collector, the survivor, late 30s–40s, male.

JOHN: Younger, an artist, the glue of his friends, early 20s, male.

CHARLES/GREG/GERALD:
- **CHARLES:** John's partner, older than John but younger than Ryan, male.
- **GREG:** Ryan's partner who dies, dances, male.
- **GERALD:** The choir director, sings "Ave Maria," male.

TOM: The janitor at the hospital where Joan works. Very blue collar, plain, early 40s, male.

FATHER JEROME: A priestly priest at the local parish, Joan's brother, late 40s–early 50s, male.

LISA: Joan's daughter, has a strong sense of justice, tends to whine, 17, female.

SHELLEY: Joan's friend, a fellow nurse, closed-minded and unknowingly cruel, 40s, female.

ANNIE: A younger nurse, very vain, a little bratty and airheaded, late 20s, female.

LINDA: Joan's friend from the choir, a very hometown kinda woman, 40s, female.

This play can be presented with the additional suggested doubling:

- **SHELLEY/LINDA**
- **LISA/ANNIE**

WE ARE A
MASTERPIECE

WHERE'S

This play takes place in Kalamazoo, Michigan.

SCENES

Scenes take place:

Graveyard
John's apartment
A hospital
Joan's house

A blank space with a prop and sound will work more efficiently than built sets.

TIME

Mostly August 1982-April 1983
and sometimes 2017.

RUN TIME

2 hours, 15 minutes

AUTHOR'S NOTE

When characters speak in sentences that have no periods, there's something unfinished about that sentence. The next sentence should not cut off the language, but it should come quickly. When sentences finish with a dash "—" this indicates an overlap. When a sentence begins with a dash, this is them finishing their previous sentence.

When a lower-case letter begins a sentence, it is the continuation of a sentence before rather than a new one.

WE ARE A
MASTERPIECE

"For we are God's masterpiece.
He has created us anew..."
—Ephesians, 2:10

"I want to hear my mother's voice. I want to see my children as children. Hands small, feet swift. Everything changes. Boy grown, father dead, daughter taller than me, weeping from a bad dream. Please stay forever, I say to the things I know. Don't go."

—Patti Smith, M Train

For
John

ACT I

PROLOGUE

2017

RYAN stands at a podium, facing us.

He shuffles a few pieces of paper, clears his throat.

Taps the microphone that makes a little screechy sound and he waits for it to quiet before he begins to speak.

RYAN: It all started with some monkeys

and a promiscuous flight attendant.

That's how the legend goes.

You've heard it.

Blood from monkeys carried the virus, some Africans cut up the monkeys to eat, got blood on their hands, seeped into their cuticles and into their veins and then a flight attendant had sex with those men and then those men had sex with other men,

depositing the virus in them like pennies into a piggybank.

Isn't that awful?

A fucked-up fairy tale, created because there were no answers.

It was like living in a horror movie, a silent serial killer picking us off one by one by ten by ten thousand,

a monster in the blood, running through the blood, shredding blood cells inside the veins

attacking all the gays.

"Only the gays." Wiping us out, not one by one but one thousand by one thousand. And none of us knew why.

I carry the dead inside my heartbeat.

I'm so old now.

My eyes have wrinkles.

My heart has wrinkles.

I thought the disease would get me. But it didn't.

And I still don't know why.

And back then, well.

None of us knew anything at all.

Lights go out.

SCENE 1

AUGUST, 1982

The sound of a shovel hitting dirt before the lights come up.

As the lights brighten, we see that we're in a graveyard. It's after midnight.

JOAN stands, watching her daughter LISA dig up the dirt, a lumpy blanket on the ground besides them.

JOAN tries to light a cigarette but she can't get a light.

JOAN: Goddammit.

> *She keeps trying before she gives up, re-pocketing the cigarette for later.*
>
> *Swats away a mosquito.*

Hey, you almost done over there?

LISA: No.

JOAN: It's getting late.

LISA: It's already late.

JOAN: I got work in the morning

LISA: And I've got school!

JOAN: So let's hurry it up

LISA: I'm going as fast as I can

JOAN: Go faster

LISA: The shovel hurts!

My hands have blisters, look

> *She shows them to JOAN, Joan shrugs.*

JOAN: You'll live.

LISA: That your medical opinion?

JOAN: Yup.

LISA: Whatever.

> *She continues digging.*
>
> *JOAN swats away another mosquito.*

JOAN: Mosquitos are eating me alive

LISA: You'll live

> *They stick their tongues out at each other.*
>
> *LISA continues digging.*

JOAN: Here's an idea.

Let's not bury him

LISA: Uh, here's a better idea,

Help me.

JOAN: I am helping you

LISA: You are not

JOAN: I'm standing watch

LISA: You're just standing there

JOAN: The doctor would've taken care of it.

Would've given him to us in a nice little box, you could've kept him on your beside dresser.

LISA: He didn't want to be burned alive

JOAN: Which is a good thing he was already dead

LISA: MOM

JOAN: What, it's true

LISA: What if someone had said all this about Pop Pop

JOAN: Pop Pop was a human, not a dog,

dogs don't have souls, they don't need to be put in the ground

LISA: He did so have a soul!

Has a soul! A soul that's free and floating in the universe and will sometimes need a place to come and rest and this was his favorite spot so I know he'll appreciate it. Big time.

> *JOAN just shakes her head.*
>
> *LISA keeps digging.*
>
> *A moment.*

JOAN: We could've just buried him in the yard, we have the space.

This place is giving me the creeps.

LISA: You're around death everyday

JOAN: That's not what's creepy.

Dirt is creepy.

The dark is creepy.

Spiders are creepy.

Death is a fact, it's not creepy.

LISA: Newsflash— spiders are also a fact.

JOAN: No they're not, they're awful

LISA: They are to some people! They're like, "Oh just some little bugs, no big deal, whatever"

JOAN: Those people are crazy

> LISA stops digging, measures the depth of the grave with her shovel.

LISA: Do you think this is deep enough?

JOAN: I dunno Lisa, I've never dug a grave for a dog before.

LISA: Can you just...?

> JOAN sighs.
>
> Glances at the hole.

JOAN: Looks good to me.

> LISA nods. Picks up the lumpy blanket.
>
> JOAN helps her lower. Together, they lower him into the hole.
>
> It's maybe not as easy as it seems.
>
> They look at the hole. Nod.
>
> Breathe.

All right, cover him up

LISA: Wait

JOAN: What?

LISA: We should

say a few words.

JOAN: He's a DOG

LISA: Please?

JOAN: Okay.

Go ahead

LISA: I can't do it!

JOAN: Why not?

LISA: I'm too upset!!

JOAN: You knew that this was part of the deal,

he was old when you got him

LISA: I know he was but I still loved him

> Beat.

JOAN: Fine.

> JOAN closes her eyes. Starts her eulogy.

Dearly beloved, we are gathered here today to remember our dearly departed Rocky Balboa.

Rocky Balboa.

JOAN (CONT'D): You really were a fighter.

You looked like you were going to die any day when we found you. Which is why I let Lisa bring you home. But to all our surprise, you lasted five years.

You might've been the oldest dog on earth. I'll regret never calling Guinness to find out.

And even though you smelled like you had died five years ago and I had to buy three Dustbusters to keep around the house to keep your disgusting hair off my uniform,

I did enjoy when you would put your head on my lap and sigh.

I related to that sigh.

I'll miss that, I think.

> *LISA holds out her hand for her MOTHER's.*
>
> *They hold hands.*

Now come on.

Let's bury this shit before we get arrested.

> *As they throw dirt on their dearly departed dog, lights go up on...*

SCENE 2

SEPTEMBER, 1982

John's apartment. CHARLES stands, facing the audience, looking at a large piece of art that none of us can see. JOHN stands behind him.

After a moment:

CHARLES: I don't get it.

JOHN: I hate you.

CHARLES: No, I mean, I like it!

JOHN: You suck

CHARLES: I just don't get it

JOHN: Greg and Ryan are going to gloat if we're late again

CHARLES: No, wait,

   just explain it to me

JOHN: No.

CHARLES: Why?

JOHN: There's nothing to explain!

   I mean, it's art. There's no answers.

CHARLES: I'm sorry, it's just.

JOHN: No, it's fine.

   You don't have to.

   I shouldn't have shown you.

CHARLES: No, I'm glad you did—

JOHN: We're gonna be late

CHARLES: It's just lunch

JOHN: and I'm hungry and Greg and Ryan want us to see their deck—

CHARLES: Greg finished the deck?

JOHN: No

CHARLES: Then what are we looking at?!

JOHN: An unfinished deck, it's a Ryan tactic, making us come over and getting excited about the deck so we can, I dunno, excite Greg into actually finishing it—

CHARLES: So we have to get excited about this deck

JOHN: About the promises of the deck

CHARLES: Got it

JOHN: Be all,

"I can just see the fourth of July barbeque now!"

CHARLES: "Oh, I can just smell the hot dogs now"

JOHN: "I can taste the sangria"

CHARLES: "I can feel the mosquitos eating me alive"

JOHN: Great so are you ready?

CHARLES: Come on, let's not—

Just talk to me.

Why'd you make it?

JOHN: Really?

Why did I make it?

CHARLES: Yeah, I mean, what's the inspiration?

JOHN: Put on your coat

CHARLES: Where did it come from?

JOHN: I'm not having this conversation

CHARLES: What, why not?

JOHN: I never know how to answer.

CHARLES: I mean, do you like get inspired by like your surroundings or like what's happening in the world, is it political or just like Something Pretty or—

JOHN: Yeah, yeah it's all those things.

CHARLES: Okay

and

JOHN: and like.

I don't know, Charles, it's.

Something I can't put words to, no matter how hard I try.

I don't know when I make the decision to make what I'm making. It just suddenly turns into what I'm making. And I suddenly recognize it.

And I say

Oh. Well. There you are.

CHARLES: Ryan should hang this in his gallery

JOHN: You don't even "get it"

CHARLES: Yeah well I'm in finance, I don't get any of this.

But I bet people would!

JOHN: Ryan'll never hang any of my stuff in his gallery, his gallery's too, I don't know, clean. My work's too chaotic for him, I honestly think it gives him an anxiety attack to look at it

>   *CHARLES walks over to JOHN, puts his hand on his chest.*

>   *Feels his heart beat.*

CHARLES: Where do you keep all that chaos, John?

I don't feel it inside you

JOHN: I pull it all out and

>   *He gestures towards the painting.*

>   *CHARLES starts taking JOHN's coat off his shoulders*

We're going to be late

CHARLES: I know

>   *A phone starts to ring.*

JOHN: Greg and Ryan are gonna complain

CHARLES: I know

>   *Ring, ring.*

JOHN: We should get that

CHARLES: In a minute

>   *Ring, ring.*

JOHN: I'm hungry

CHARLES: Me, too.

>   *They start to kiss. They kiss as the lights go down on them and up on the next scene.*

SCENE 3

SEPTEMBER, 1982

The lunchroom of the hospital. SHELLEY sits, eating lunch.

ANNIE is reading a fashion magazine.

JOAN enters, sits down right in front of SHELLEY.

JOAN: Your lunch smells.

> *SHELLEY offers her some. JOAN takes it, eats it.*

Oh, that's good

SHELLEY: I know

Got the recipe from the back of a French Onion packet

JOAN: No kidding

SHELLEY: Yeah, I had a bunch of French Onion packets left over from the party, I knew I wasn't going to need as much as I bought but they were on sale and what was I supposed to do, not buy them, they were on sale!

JOAN: Sales are dangerous

SHELLEY: Right?

and I mean, I knew, I was like "What the hell am I supposed to do with these now, throw another party, I can't just throw another party, it's too much work"

JOAN: I know

SHELLEY: All the shopping, cooking, planning, it's just too much

JOAN: I know, that's why I don't throw parties

SHELLEY: so I was looking at all these packets of French Onion mixes and was all ready to put them in the back of the cabinet and forget about them and I happened to look at the back of one of the packets and bam, there's a recipe and the lights from Heaven shined down and a chorus of angels started singing

ANNIE: You didn't invite me to your party

SHELLEY: It was just a small party

ANNIE: I like parties

SHELLEY: I'll keep that in mind

> *ANNIE goes back to reading the magazine.*
>
> *TOM enters with lunch.*
>
> *Walks over to a table, sits at it.*

TOM: Hi all.

JOAN: Hi Tom.

The other LADIES half-heartedly greet him.

SHELLEY: Best part?

  Different recipes.

  Gonna keep me busy for a while.

JOAN: Always trust the sale

SHELLEY: Always trust the sale!

They clink whatever beverages they're drinking.

ANNIE: Well, it's official.

  My hair needs to be bigger

JOAN: Your hair looks fine

ANNIE: Yeah, exactly.

  It looks *fine.*

  It doesn't look *great.*

SHELLEY: You shouldn't read those things

JOAN: Yeah, next thing you know you'll want shoulderpads in your uniform

ANNIE: So?

JOAN: Nobody here cares what you look like, Annie

ANNIE: You never know

SHELLEY: This isn't Dallas, Annie!

  People come here to either get better or die, nobody's going to marry you

ANNIE: You never know!

  Joan met her husband here!

Awkward silence.

  Oh, sorry,

  your divorced husband

JOAN: Yes

ANNIE: So???

JOAN: So never marry a man you meet at the hospital

SHELLEY: Especially not a doctor, they're all playboys

ANNIE: How can they be, they're doctors, they have to always tell the truth

SHELLEY: That's lawyers, Annie

ANNIE: Dr. Howell is really cute

JOAN: Dr. Howell?

SHELLEY: He's so faggy

ANNIE: He's mysterious!

You don't have to be so judgmental, I haven't said anything about the fact your apparently amazing lunch smells like vomit

SHELLEY: Vomit?!

JOAN: It doesn't smell that bad

ANNIE: Oh yeah, then why do I smell vomit?

JOAN: It smells like onions

SHELLEY: I have no idea what you're talking about

TOM: Yeah, I've smelled my fair share of vomit and I can't say anything in this cafeteria smells like vomit, currently.

> *They all awkwardly look at him and politely smile.*

ANNIE: Oh wait, sorry,

no, that's me, I still have vomit in my hair

SHELLEY: Yeah, go ahead and make your hair bigger, see how much more vomit you can collect in it

ANNIE: Argh, I thought I got it all out

JOAN: Go rinse it!

ANNIE: I already did

JOAN: So do it again, Annie!

SHELLEY: For the love of God, you have vomit in your hair!

ANNIE: It's not that big a deal!

JOAN: Go wash your hair!

SHELLEY: Disgusting!

ANNIE: God, fine!

> *She stomps her way out.*

> *SHELLEY and JOAN burst out laughing.*

JOAN: Oh my God, Annie

SHELLEY: I know

JOAN: How does she make it through a day?

SHELLEY: I don't know

> *Their laughter subsides.*

TOM: They're going to discontinue Aspen.

> *An awkward silence.*

SHELLEY: Aspen's a city

TOM: No, the pop.

TOM (CONT'D): Tastes like cheap champagne and apples.

Dunno why they'd do away with it.

JOAN: I've never had Aspen.

TOM: You don't know what you're missing.

He balls up his lunch, throws it out, and leaves.

SHELLEY: He's so WEIRD, why does he eat in here, doesn't he have a broom closet he can curl up inside

JOAN: Oh, you're so bad

They giggle together.

SHELLEY: So.

Have you heard from him?

JOAN: Who, Tom?

SHELLEY: Joanie

JOAN: No.

SHELLEY: Even though the judge said

JOAN: Yeah, I know.

I know.

But.

It's all right it's.

Not a big deal.

SHELLEY: Joan

JOAN: He's been out of work since the divorce, what is he supposed to pay me with, blood? That's okay, I don't need it and he can keep it

SHELLEY: He owes you like

JOAN: Sometimes I wonder if I should've stayed

SHELLEY: Don't go talking crazy

JOAN: Jerome thinks I should've stayed

SHELLEY: Well he kinda has to think that.

Right?

He is a priest.

JOAN: Yeah.

She puts her hand over JOAN's.

SHELLEY: But you're his sister.

JOAN: Well.

Can't choose your family, right?

SHELLEY hugs JOAN.

SHELLEY: You've still got me.

JOAN: Yeah, I guess I do.

How do I get rid of you?

SHELLEY swats JOAN.

SHELLEY: You can't!

You're stuck with me.

JOAN: You promise?

SHELLEY: I promise.

They side hug one another as the lights come up on a different area of the hospital.

SCENE 4

SEPTEMBER, 1982

RYAN is sitting in a waiting room, trying to read a magazine.

He closes it, puts it down next to him.

Sits for a moment.

Picks it back up, tries to read it again.

JOHN and CHARLES enter.

RYAN immediately jumps up,

Hugs them.

They all hug each other, the desperate hug of brothers.

JOHN breaks away.

JOHN: How are you

RYAN: Fine, fine, I'm fine.

CHARLES: Has the doctor been out

RYAN: Yes

CHARLES: Great, what'd he say

RYAN: I don't know

CHARLES: Meaning

RYAN: I mean I don't know, I don't know

he won't tell me—

I'm not family

CHARLES: I'm gonna bribe a nurse

RYAN: You don't have to do that

CHARLES: No, it's fine

RYAN: I'm sure he's...

CHARLES: No, it's fine, I've done it before, nurses and nuns, they're easy to bribe

RYAN: Come on, Charles, don't—

JOHN: Just let him do it, he's going to do it

RYAN: It's really—

CHARLES: I'll be right back!

He sprints out of the room.

JOHN: You know Charles,

just wants to prove to himself he can do it

RYAN: He really doesn't have to, I'm sure he's going to be fine, right?

JOHN: Of course!

People faint all the time

RYAN: Yeah.

JOHN: and you said he had a cold, probably just dehydrated or something

RYAN: Sure.

It's fine.

He's fine.

> *A moment of silence.*
> *RYAN picks up the magazine.*
> *Puts it down.*

Sorry about lunch

JOHN: Lunch doesn't matter

RYAN: Sure.

JOHN: Unless— are you hungry? I can get you some chips, cookies or something, I'm sure there's something —

RYAN: I was at a wedding— Josie and Kevins'

JOHN: Oh, how was it?!

RYAN: Beautiful

JOHN: I wanted to go, who has a wedding in New Mexico

RYAN: Pain in the ass to get there but I think her family

JOHN: Oh, right

RYAN: they have a house out there so

JOHN: sure sure

RYAN: Gorgeous.

Acres and acres of land, they had it outdoors, weather held

JOHN: I always worry about that

RYAN: I know but it was good, the weather was beautiful, the wedding was beautiful, she was beautiful, he was beautiful, everything was beautiful.

There were all these flowers, I kept thinking I have to remember to tell Greggie about all these flowers, I asked what kind they were, not the kind you normally see at weddings, they were something like cacti flowers, nothing I'd ever seen before and you know Greggie, always outdoors, always looking for a new thing to plant, he's always so smug about it too, thinks he's an encyclopedia of flowers, that he knows every flower that ever sprouted from God's green earth and I saw this kind and

now I don't remember what the flower was.

RYAN (CONT'D): I took pictures.

Haven't even gotten the film developed

JOHN: I can do it

RYAN: It's all right John

JOHN: No, it's really no problem at all, do you want me to go

RYAN: It was a really nice wedding.

I danced.

Danced myself into a sweat.

The band was great and everyone was dancing and I was dancing and.

I was so excited to get home. To tell him about the wedding and the flowers and I called him from the airport and I said

You still have that cold, huh

and he said

Feeling better today,

thinking about getting the garden ready for winter and

he said he was feeling better and

all I wanted to do was see him and I came home and said I'm home and he was.

Covered in sweat.

Lying on the floor.

He had a cough when I left and.

He's never going to finish that deck

JOHN: Of course he will

RYAN: He's not okay

> *JOHN holds his hand as CHARLES comes out.*
>
> *They look at CHARLES.*
>
> *He opens and closes his mouth.*
>
> *RYAN cries.*
>
> *They comfort him as the sound of an organ starts to play, and suddenly we're in...*

SCENE 5

OCTOBER, 1982

Church on a Sunday! All the God-fearing folks' favorite day of the week!!

FATHER JEROME is standing up on the altar, he's giving his homily.

He is a very animated priest, generally works himself into a state of enthusiasm and paces back and forth, pointing at his congregation when he mentions them by name.

FATHER JEROME: God is Awesome.

Do you know what that word means?

Does anyone REMEMBER what that word means? It's become so watered down, it's become nothing but slang, you hear the kids, out there with your ripped jeans and your, your big hair —like you, is it really necessary for your hair to be that big, Ms. Jones?— and you walk down the street, popping your gum and chatting about the latest movie or band or television program and say, what do you say, you say

He does a valley girl-esque impressions:

"Oh, hey Sarah, hey did you hear about that Awesome new show"

and Sarah will say

"Oh yah, I do know, Sally, I know it's so so so Awesome,"

just throwing that word around like it weighs as much as cotton candy!

He gets more serious here, really breaking down the word for his congregation.

It excites him to share this news with them.

Awe— to be in awe means to be completely and utterly and undeniably overWHELMED. When Moses parted the red sea, that was AWESOME. When Jesus resisted temptation in the desert after forty days— FORTY DAYS! Some of you can't last forty minutes— That. was AWE. SOME. When God created Adam and Eve, effectively bringing life to this world, THAT was AWESOME.

Movies and bubble gum and hair styles are NOT awesome.

They're cool, they're fine, they're interesting— they are not. Awesome.

GOD is awesome. Don't roll your eyes at me, Mr. Tucker, you forget I can see you all, I am 20 inches above you, I can see you reading a novel, Ms. Peters, you better put that away,

I'm sorry I'm not as entertaining as God is, I'm sorry I'm not as AWESOME as God is but you know what, I don't have to be.

FATHER JEROME (CONT'D): And you, you don't have to listen to a word I say, you can say, "But Father Jerome, why does this word matter, why are you so upset about that word"

but then, why are you here?

Lights fade down on him as they raise on...

SCENE 6

OCTOBER, 1982

After church; JOAN is trying to leave but LINDA sees her.

She hasn't seen her in such a long time!

This is very exciting!!

LINDA: Joanie?

Joanie Stewart, is that you?

JOAN: Yes, hi, Linda.

LINDA: HI!

JOAN: Hi.

LINDA: I haven't seen you in—

JOAN: I know!

I know, I...

Choir sounded nice today.

LINDA: Oh, no

JOAN: Yes

LINDA: Do you really think so

JOAN: I do

Sounded great.

LINDA: Oh, well

JOAN: Just like angels

LINDA: We were okay, we'd sound better if people actually showed up for practice but, you know how it goes!

JOAN: Sure.

LINDA: You remember that life!

JOAN: Yup

LINDA: We miss you in the altos— there's only three of us now and one of us is little Margaret and God help her, she can't remember her name let alone a harmony, she's 90 years old now, if you can believe it— and you know Bettyann, she's just there for the cookies and the gossip so it's really just me up there, singing as loud as I can go and

do you know Bettyann had the nerve to say something about how loud I am, well, you remember how she is, didn't even say it to my face, overheard her in the parking lot complaining to Liz, "Oh that Linda thinks she's the tops the way she sings, so loud,"

and I went right up to her and said

LINDA (CONT'D): Excuse me, I'm only singing loud so God can hear the altos what's the use of a harmony if you can't hear it, I mean what's the use of a choir,

I'm sure Gerald would adore it if you came back

JOAN: Yeah.

LINDA: We'd all adore it!

Awkward pause.

JOAN: Sure.

I should really get—

LINDA: It's so good to see you, Joanie!

It's really been a while!

JOAN: I've just

been going to a different church

LINDA: You don't want to see your brother?

JOAN: Oh, no, that's not the—

LINDA: I think he's just fabulous

JOAN: He's pretty.

Something

LINDA: Ties everything together so beautifully, speaks the truth

JOAN: Yeah, he's great.

He's

LINDA: Awesome!

She laughs at her own joke.

The silence that follows is just.

So awkward.

He is Awesome, right?

JOAN: It was nice seeing you—

LINDA: Oh, do you know what I've been meaning to call you,

for that recipe, that bread thing, you brought it into Bible study that one time—

JOAN: Oh, sure— which, what was—

LINDA: You know, it was a bread thing

JOAN: Sure

LINDA: kinda tasted like autumn in a baked good

JOAN: Oh, yeah, sure, the banana bread

LINDA: Yes! That's it!

Such a nice fall dessert, like if fall had a flavor it would be that bread

JOAN: I mean,

it's probably just the.

Cinnamon but

LINDA: I swear, if autumn had a flavor, it would be cinnamon

They both consider this for a moment.

That might be really true.

Anyway, I have a potluck coming up, so.

I'd love to bring it!

JOAN: Sure, sure just give me a call

LINDA: I don't have your new number—

JOAN: No, I'm at the same number—

LINDA: But— Jack?

JOAN: He is not at the same number.

LINDA: Oh, wow.

How modern!

JOAN: Well, it is my house!

So!

LINDA: Well, great!

Here I was just assuming—

JOAN: Well, you know what they say about assumptions

LINDA: Sure

JOAN: they make an ass! Out of you and me.

LINDA is like wait was that a joke or are you calling me an...

JOAN is like no, I'm calling you an ass, lady.

LINDA: I'll just give you a call, then.

JOAN: Sure, sounds good.

Starts to leave.

LINDA: I miss you, Joanie.

JOAN: Just.

Give me a call.

Okay?

LINDA: Sure.

I'll call you.

Lights shift.

SCENE 7

OCTOBER, 1982

The nurses' station at a hospital. JOAN is standing there, filling out paperwork.

SHELLEY and ANNIE are whispering with one another.

We hear and see them say and do:

SHELLEY & ANNIE: Rock paper scissors

ANNIE chooses paper; SHELLEY chooses rock.

SHELLEY *(simultaneously)*: Shit

ANNIE *(simultaneously)*: Yes

  Go again

ANNIE: No

SHELLEY: Best two out of three

ANNIE: I already won

SHELLEY: So let's go again

ANNIE: Because...

SHELLEY: Because

ANNIE: Because you lost

SHELLEY: Yeah, so?

TOM enters, mopping.

He starts to eavesdrop on the scene.

JOAN: Who's going into Room 102?

SHELLEY: We're figuring it out right now

JOAN: What do you mean you're figuring it out

ANNIE: Yeah, we already figured it out, paper beats rock, you lost, you gotta go look at him

SHELLEY: And I said,

  "Best two out of three"

JOAN: Does somebody want to tell me what's going on?

ANNIE: It's the gay cancer

SHELLEY: GRID.

Beat. Oh.

TOM: Gay cancer?

ANNIE: Don't you have to mop something

TOM: I am

JOAN: Yeah, that's what it is, been all over the news

SHELLEY: Just came in

ANNIE: Yeah, Doc Graves says they're fighting off reporters— first case in Kalamazoo

SHELLEY: So go be a part of history, Annie

ANNIE: You be part of history, I'm gonna take a smoke break

SHELLEY: I'm older than you!

ANNIE: Yeah, whose fault is that?!

JOAN: All right, enough!

I'll do it.

> *She grabs a mask from SHELLY's hand.*

SHELLEY: Joan

JOAN: What

SHELLEY: Thank you.

JOAN: Somebody has to do it.

> *JOAN puts her mask on. Opens the door to the room and enters.*
>
> *Lights up on...*

SCENE 8

OCTOBER, 1982

A hospital room.

On the other side of the stage, JOHN paints.

JOAN enters the hospital room.

GREG is lying on the bed, barely breathing. We can hear the beeping and whirling of hospital machines.

She approaches him. Takes a look at his chart. Gets to work.

He stirs.

GREG: Mom, Mom.

Mom.

Mom

The door opens, RYAN enters.

Mom.

RYAN: Hi.

JOAN: Hello

RYAN: I was just.

I'm visiting—

JOAN: It's fine.

RYAN: Was in the bathroom—

JOAN: It's fine

RYAN: drinking a lot of coffee

kinda running on it these days.

Like gasoline.

Beat.

Can you tell me anything? About him?

JOAN: I can release that information to family, are you family?

RYAN: Sure, we're brothers.

JOAN gives him a look.

JOAN: Is his mother coming?

I can tell her...

RYAN: No.

Of course not.

They haven't spoken since.

RYAN (CONT'D): For years.

So.

JOAN: You might want to tell her how sick he is.

RYAN: I have

JOAN: I'm sure if she knew—

RYAN: We tried to call her.

She knows he's dying.

She's not coming.

JOAN: Sure

RYAN: You don't believe me

She's not coming.

But I'm here.

I'm here.

So tell me?

JOAN: I can't.

She begins to leave.

RYAN: Do you know anything?

Like, why this is happening?

JOAN: Why would I know anything like that—

RYAN: I mean

You're a nurse, right?

JOAN: Yes but.

We don't have.

We're not wizards, we don't know what's going on

RYAN: You know nothing, doctors know nothing, there's nothing anyone can do, nobody knows anything except that he's dying.

I mean, I'm no doctor but.

How can you know that he's dying,

but not know why he's dying?

Maybe it's because none of you really know what you're doing.

Or maybe because it's just a bunch of fags getting it nobody gives a shit.

Right?

JOAN: I don't know what you want me to do,

there's nothing I can do

       Beat.

GREG: Mom.

  Mom.

       JOAN starts to exit.

       RYAN touches GREG's forehead and speaks.

RYAN: He's endless. You know? Even if I had a lifetime to talk about everything he is I wouldn't be able to cover even a fraction of it. Like how he laughs or how he breathes or how he farts or how in the middle of the night I could reach over to him and feel him there and how my heart could feel so complete? It could feel so complete and now it's going to feel so incomplete? And his skin. And his breaths. And him. And he didn't always look like this but for some reason he's more beautiful to me now than I ever saw.

  I miss him already and he's not even gone yet.

       JOAN opens and closes her mouth.

       Leaves it closed.

       Begins to leave.

       Stops.

JOAN: How do you take it?

RYAN: What?

JOAN: Your coffee, how do you take it?

       Pause.

  I take it black.

RYAN: Light and sweet.

       She nods.

       Leaves.

       RYAN looks at GREG. He crawls into bed with him.

       Holds him close.

       JOAN re-enters, holding a coffee cup.

       Sees them.

       Stops.

       Puts the coffee on the nightstand.

       Leaves without a word.

       He holds onto him as the lights dim on the scene.

SCENE 9

OCTOBER, 1982

JOHN enters the hospital, by the nurse's station.

He's holding flowers.

Approaches JOAN.

JOHN: Excuse me, do you know what room Greg Smith is in?

JOAN: Room 102

JOHN: Great, thanks

He begins to leave.

JOAN: You can't bring those in there

JOHN: Oh, right, because it's too faggy to bring a man flowers, right, how dare you, how fucking dare—

JOAN gives him a glare

JOAN: He's too sick.

JOHN: Oh.

JOAN: Yeah.

JOHN: Shit.

I didn't know

JOAN: Obviously.

Beat.

JOHN: Here.

You take them.

JOAN: Me?

JOHN: Sure.

JOAN: Well.

Okay.

He hands her the flowers.

Thank you.

JOHN: No problem.

JOAN: Here.

You'll need this.

Hands him a mask.

JOHN: This'll protect me?

JOAN: It's for him.

JOHN: Oh.

Sure.

> *JOHN holds the mask.*

JOAN: His— someone's with him

JOHN: Ryan?

JOAN: I didn't ask

JOHN: So I shouldn't—

JOAN: No, you can go on in.

JOHN: All right.

Sure.

Okay.

> *He starts to head towards the door.*
> *Stops.*

How's he.

Is he okay?

JOAN: He's really sick.

JOHN: I know it just.

Happened really fast.

We were supposed to get lunch.

The four of us. But we never made it.

And now he's here and.

Flowers.

Why would I bring him flowers?

It was stupid

JOAN: Not stupid.

They're pretty.

They're beautiful.

They just might make him sicker.

His immune system is in tatters. Anything can make him sicker. Bringing flowers, it's a nice thing. Bringing yourself is even better. Go on inside. Instead of just hanging out here.

> *JOHN hesitates.*

JOHN: I'm scared

Isn't that horrible?

JOAN: No, you can be scared.

That's not horrible.

If you don't go inside because you're scared.

That's horrible.

He nods.

JOHN: I'm John.

JOAN: Joan.

JOHN: We're twins.

JOAN gives him a look.

Joan and John.

Sounds like a TV show.

JOAN: I don't watch TV.

JOHN: You should, there's a lot of great shows.

JOAN: My daughter started watching some new one, Cheers?

JOHN: I don't know it

JOAN: She says it's funny but it just looks like a show about a bunch of alcoholics who hang out at a bar.

JOHN: I dunno, that sounds pretty funny.

Beat.

I've never seen anybody dying before.

JOAN: It's not easy.

But it's worse if you don't go in.

JOHN: Okay.

I'll do anything for him.

He's more of a brother than any of my brothers ever were.

JOAN: Family's important.

JOHN: Yeah, it is.

But sometimes they kill you.

After a moment.

JOAN: Yeah, they can.

JOHN puts on his mask, enters the room.

SHELLEY walks over.

SHELLEY: Thanks again, Joanie

JOAN: It really was no problem.

SHELLEY: Those cases really give me the heebie jeebies,

Ugh yuck.

I thought it would stay in New York City and San Francisco, never thought it would make it out to Kalamazoo. Thought we were safe out here.

Thanks again for bailing me out.

Gives JOAN a squeeze.

JOAN: Did someone try to contact his mother?

SHELLEY: Sure

JOAN: The guy he's with, Ryan, he said she's not coming.

His mother.

SHELLEY: Probably not

JOAN: But.

He's dying

SHELLEY: Yeah but.

You can't blame her for not coming, can you?

It's his own fault.

JOAN: I guess.

SHELLEY: It's disgusting, really,

I don't know what I'd do if Richie thought he was—

You know what, I don't even want to think about it, just thank God he isn't

JOAN: Right

SHELLEY: Hey, let's grab a drink after work today.

JOAN: Sure, that sounds great, Shelley.

That sounds great.

Lights up on...

SCENE 10

OCTOBER, 1982

John's apartment. He and CHARLES sit, side by side.

After a moment:

JOHN: So.

  You got it, too?

> *CHARLES: Nods.*

JOHN: Oh.

> *Beat.*

  Okay.

> *Beat.*

CHARLES: It's a plague.

JOHN: A plague

CHARLES: Yes, a plague.

  A gay plague.

  A biblical plague

  From God.

JOHN: No, Charles, don't go getting all crazy

CHARLES: I mean, it's not that crazy, I don't think it's crazy,

  really, what's crazy about it.

  It's only the gays, right, that's what they're saying, GRID, right, gay-related immune deficiency, that's what it's called, more cases everyday, more and more cases every single day,

  it's kinda, this is kinda what God does, isn't it?

  God killed a bunch of children to make a point, what's to stop him from killing a bunch of fags, too

JOHN: All right, so logically, if we look at this logically, you're going to believe that not only is God real, but that after millions of years on Earth he's decided to shake things up a bit by exterminating queers

CHARLES: Why not?

  Why not, right, if that's what they're already out there, saying, why can't I say it, too, sure. It's God, capital G God, then I know who to be angry at.

  It's not fair, John,

  I just.

  Can't believe I.

CHARLES (CONT'D): I just have a cough and.

I have this big project we're working on and all I can keep thinking is that I won't be there to finish it.

JOHN: You can't think that way

CHARLES: Nobody at work knows, you know?

They just think I'm some kind of bachelor living some kind of crazy bachelor life, that I spend my weekends out, going to concerts and picking up women, that's what all the guys at work think,

they don't know,

they don't know that I spend every weekend with you and that we buy groceries and let the dishes pile up in the sink and talk about buying a new couch in a darker shade so it'll be easier to hide our food stains, they don't know any of that,

I hide that, I've had to hide that and pretend that I'm not this and

now everyone'll know and it won't matter because I'll be dead.

I'm going to die, John.

            Beat.

JOHN: I know.

CHARLES: I don't want to.

JOHN: I don't want you to.

But.

I know that I love you.

I know that I'm not going to leave you.

CHARLES: Do you promise?

JOHN: Yes, I promise.

I'm not going anywhere.

            They hold each other tight.

CHARLES: You're just being nice to me because I'm dying.

JOHN: So what if I am, doesn't make it less true.

            They hug one another.

            JOHN goes to kiss CHARLES, but Charles stops him

CHARLES: I don't know if it's—

            JOHN kisses him anyway.

JOHN: I don't care.

            They stay hugging one another for a moment.

So. What should we do?

SCENE 11

2017/1982

RYAN's speech, continued.

While he gives this speech, we watch CHARLES get sicker and sicker, eventually winding up in the hospital bed by the end of it.

RYAN: Touch heals.

That's something that's been discovered in the past few years— the power of touch helps to increase health and soothe the soul, even for the dying.

Especially for the dying.

This is something that's just been discovered but it's always been true.

Being treated with dignity, being treated like a human— that also helps, too.

Not just psychologically, but physically. It's been proven in the last few years that these things— touching another person's skin, treating them with empathy— that it helps to heal them.

Doctors looked at us like we were jumbo-sized lab rats, clinical with a hint of disgust. We weren't human. We were a question to be answered, a puzzle to be solved but not at the costs of their health. They didn't see us.

I would see these souls, these giant souls trapped inside these little men. They would enter the hospital, all pumped up and full and deflate like balloons, right before my eyes, most of them covered in spots like leopards or lepers or.

Don't be fooled. Death isn't pretty or romantic or poetic, it's beyond gross and horrible and so was it beyond gross and horrible the way we were treated.

I am not a doctor or a nurse and it wasn't my job, it shouldn't have been any of our jobs to watch our friends die. But I had to learn how to watch my friends die.

That's something nobody should need to learn how to do.

> *CHARLES is in his hospital bed, JOHN beside him as we begin.*

SCENE 12

NOVEMBER, 1982

The hospital, Charles' room.

JOHN is pacing.

He opens up the door to look out in the hall—

Sees a tray of food was left outside the door.

He picks it up, angry.

Brings it inside the room.

Contemplates waking up CHARLES.

Decides to let him sleep.

TOM enters.

TOM: Hi.

JOHN: Hi

TOM starts to clean.

What are you doing?

TOM: Oh, I'm mopping.

JOHN: Yeah, I can see that—

TOM: This is room 302, right?

JOHN: Yeah

TOM: Okay, good.

I was worried I had the wrong vomit

JOHN: Oh.

I'm sorry it's just.

TOM: You're an artist, huh

JOHN: What?

TOM: You have paint. In your cuticles.

JOHN: Oh. Yeah.

TOM: Yeah, I'm very observant.

I like to observe things.

JOHN: That's... cool.

TOM: Artists forget to wash their hands.

And forget to clean up after themselves.

It's a fact.

You have too much daydreams up there or something.

TOM (CONT'D): Your minds work different from the common man.

I read it in a book once,

I read a lot?

I think that's why I'm so observant.

Mostly self-help books,

I don't like fiction,

outer space, right? Who cares?!

And I don't like biographies or memoirs—

I mean, I just don't really care to read about a celebrity's life story,

no mater how humble they pretend to be, they never really are, you know?

So that leaves self-help books,

I read them all,

even ones that aren't very helpful,

or ones that don't apply to me, necessarily,

they're almost like fiction except they're grounded in reality,

in truth,

so that makes them not fiction and I like them.

What's his name?

JOHN: What?

Oh, Charles

TOM: How's he doing?

JOHN: Not great.

TOM: Yeah.

TOM keeps mopping.

JOHN: Aren't you scared?

TOM: Oh, sure.

The Russians are gonna bomb us any day, do you know about this?

They did a special on the news—

JOHN: No, I mean.

You saw the signs? On the door

TOM: Oh.

Yeah. But.

TOM (CONT'D): Someone's sick.

So.

Here I am!

Goes back to mopping the floor.

JOHN: Thank you.

TOM: Hey, it's no problem.

It's my job.

I mean, things are either infectious or they're not, you know?

That's my motto.

JOHN: I like your motto.

TOM: It should be on a t-shirt, right?

They have some weird things on t-shirts.

I bet I could be famous if I tried.

Weird beat where he thinks about being famous.

JOHN: Nurses won't even.

Come in with food, you know?

Just leave it outside, don't even know it's there.

One came in, she wore gloves and like three masks—

Wouldn't even look at me, like she could get it if she looked too long.

TOM: Yeah, well, that's stupid.

Fear makes people stupid, I think.

That's another motto.

JOHN: You sure you're not a writer?

With all these mottos

TOM: Oh, nah, I'm too concrete for all that.

What do you paint?

JOHN: Oh, I don't know.

TOM: I knew a guy, he used to paint boats.

Just boats, all day, but like they weren't always on the water,

sometimes they were in lava

or sometimes they were in the street

and sometimes,

they were flying.

TOM (CONT'D): Can you imagine that?

   Flying boats!

   Through clouds!

   Through outer space!!

JOHN: That sounds

   inventive.

TOM: And what,

   there's a guy famous

   for painting soup cans!

   AND

   there's a guy

   who's famous for painting

   COLOR!

   Just a block of color on a piece of paper.

   Isn't that wild?

JOHN: Yeah, that's wild.

TOM: So what do you paint?

   Houses?

                Laughs at his own joke.

                JOHN starts laughing, too.

JOHN: I shouldn't be laughing this hard

TOM: Hey, it's a good joke!

   I'm a funny guy

JOHN: You are!

   You really are.

   Thanks.

   I didn't get your name?

TOM: Oh, I'm Tom.

   Janitor.

JOHN: I'm John.

   And this is—

TOM: Charles, yeah.

   You mentioned.

JOHN: Yeah.

I guess I did.

> *Slight beat.*

I think I'm trying to paint truth?

Which sounds just so.

Pretentious.

Right?

But, really, I think that's what I'm trying to paint.

I think I'm just trying to capture truth.

And put it on a canvas.

My truth.

I think I'm chasing my truth.

Trying to create a masterpiece before.

TOM: Before what?

> *Realizes he means before he dies.*

Oh!

Oh, yeah, sure.

That's a good goal.

JOHN: Yeah.

> *TOM is done cleaning.*
> *I mean, he's been done for a bit but.*
> *He likes the company.*

Thanks again.

For.

Coming in.

Taking care of—

TOM: Hey, no problem.

My pleasure, guy.

> *He leaves.*
> *JOHN looks around the room.*
> *It's quiet without TOM.*
> *JOAN enters.*

JOAN: Sorry we're—

John?

JOHN: Joan.

JOAN: Is this your—

JOHN nods.

JOAN: I'm so sorry.

SCENE 13

NOVEMBER, 1982

JOAN's house.

LISA enters.

LISA: Wow, you're actually home

JOAN: Yes, I live here

LISA: Yeah, no I know but I mean.

   Whatever, never mind.

JOAN: I'm exhausted, do you mind ordering pizza?

   Just cheese, I don't want any of your weird toppings ruining the cheese—

LISA: Did you get my note?

JOAN: No

LISA: I left it on the kitchen table, I need 20 dollars

JOAN: For what

LISA: Yearbook pictures

JOAN: I don't have 20 dollars

LISA: Well then I guess you don't need pictures of me

JOAN: I swear, that school thinks I'm made of money

LISA: No, they think that you're growing money trees instead of apple trees that you can just wait until they bloom and you can pick off 20 dollars at your leisure

JOAN: That would be nice.

LISA: I mean, we can also not have yearbook photos of me, I am also totally fine with that

JOAN: There's no way I'm not getting those photos

LISA: I'm so ugly though

JOAN: You're gorgeous

LISA: Mommmm

> *They have a nice mother/daughter moment.*
>
> *After another moment*

You haven't been home for dinner in forever

JOAN: I know.

   Things are just.

   A little crazy at work right now.

LISA: Yeah well, things are also really crazy at school right now, they're trying to censor us, Mom, they're trying to censor the newspaper, they said that there's not enough money in the budget to keep it going but I know for a fact— a FACT— that the football team JUST got money for a new MASCOT UNIFORM. They have enough money for an oversized rodent costume, but they don't have enough money for PAPER and for INK, they just don't want us exposing the truth

JOAN: What's there to expose

LISA: A lot, Mom, there is a lot to expose

JOAN: Well, I'm sorry that's all happening

LISA: High school is hard and it sucks.

JOAN: Sounds about right.

Order the pizza, I'm just going to change—

LISA: You're going to come see Peter Pan though, right?

JOAN: You're in Peter Pan?

LISA: Uh, yeah, Mom, I AM Peter Pan

JOAN: Peter Pan's a boy

LISA: Wow, you really are culturally illiterate

JOAN: Sounds about right.

LISA: It's going to be next weekend and the weekend after and also a few performances after school on the weekday and a matinee performance on Thursday, you're coming, right?

JOAN: I don't know, Lisa, we're working crazy hours, a couple of people from work haven't been coming in

LISA: You're busy taking care of the gays.

That's what Uncle Jerome says.

JOAN: Oh yeah?

LISA: Yeah you're not too busy doing your regular work, you're like going out of your way to take care of gay guys which is pretty gross

JOAN: Stop it, Lisa

LISA: What, it is

JOAN: We're understaffed at work.

I need to be there.

I will try to make your play that I didn't know about but I cannot promise you I'll be there. Okay?

Order the pizza.

Begins to walk away.

LISA: I'm asking Dad.

JOAN: No you aren't

LISA: Why not

JOAN: Because I said you're not

LISA: Well if you're not going to go then I think that I have a right to have at least one parent present and if it's not going to be you I think it should be Dad as he is the other parent in this situation!

JOAN: I said.

No.

LISA: I don't care, I already called him and he's coming and he's excited and he said he's going to bring me flowers

JOAN: Lisa, you can't just— you absolutely can't just call your father without telling me

LISA: Yes I can, he's my DAD

JOAN: That doesn't matter

LISA: It's not my fault Daddy left you

JOAN: Go to your room, Lisa

LISA: That's not fair, Mom!

JOAN: I know, I'm not fair, nothing's fair, go to your room, now!

I don't want to hear it anymore!

LISA: I hate you!

She runs away.

JOAN: Goddammit.

SCENE 14

NOVEMBER, 1982

A hospital room.

Someone has just died. The bed is wrinkled.

Nobody has been in there to clean.

JOAN enters.

She begins to clean.

TOM enters.

He begins to mop.

TOM: What are you doing for Thanksgiving?

JOAN: What?

TOM: I'm going to my sister's, she's out in Chicago. Probably driving out early on Thanksgiving Day, get there in time to watch the parade with my nieces if I time it out right.

Crossing state lines, you know. It's more fun than driving local, better for license plate bingo— you ever play? I write up a bingo sheet with different states and every time I see a license plate from a different state I cross it off until I get all them across or diagonal or what have you and I shout, "Bingo Bango!"

I win every time.

Especially with holiday traffic, that's the best time to play it, lots of cars out on the highway—

JOAN: Oh.

Thanksgiving is next week.

I forgot.

TOM: Yeah.

My sister makes a great sweet potato thing. I'm not sure what it's called, but it's got sweet potatoes and marshmallows and yams?

What is the difference between a yam and a sweet potato, anyway?

Ponders this question for a bit.

I can bring you back some if you like.

JOAN: Thank you.

TOM: Yeah, sure no problem

JOAN: No not about the yams

TOM: Sweet potatoes

JOAN: This.

JOAN (CONT'D): This, thank you.

    For helping.

TOM: Hey, no problem.

JOAN: Nobody else wants to come in here—

TOM: I know.

    That's a little silly, I think.

JOAN: It's something.

TOM: It's not right.

JOAN: You know what.

    That's true.

                    They clean together.

    It'll just be me and Lisa this year.

    My daughter.

    Maybe we'll order pizza.

TOM: Hey, that counts as a pie, right?

JOAN: Yes.

    It sure does.

               They finish cleaning together.

SCENE 15

DECEMBER, 1982

Joan's car. RYAN is sitting in the passenger seat, staring out.

He wears a winter coat, seems a little cold, maybe.

He sits like that for a moment in silence, like a zombie staring out.

JOAN enters. She's holding a box.

Opens the car door on the driver's side, gets in.

Gives RYAN the box.

RYAN holds the box.

Hugs it to him.

There's a moment of silence.

JOAN: I got you a candy bar.

> *She takes it out of her purse.*

Almond Joy.

> *RYAN: Doesn't say anything.*

Not my favorite.

I actually, I don't like nuts in candy, I prefer caramel, just straight caramel and chocolate, no nuts getting in the way.

But they didn't really have much— their vending machine was half empty, that whole place was half empty, full of people with half a brain and—

Honestly, how hard can it be to keep a vending machine stocked—

RYAN: He didn't want to be burned.

> *Beat.*

JOAN: I'm sorry, it's just.

What we need to do—

RYAN: But it's not what he wanted.

JOAN: It's too dangerous—

RYAN: Says who, says you?

JOAN: Says the CDC

RYAN: Great, so they can say that, and?

What else can they tell you, what else do they know,

they're so sure of that so

what else do they know?

JOAN: We still don't know enough about it—

RYAN: So they know a lot of nothing, so they don't know if letting him be buried would have been okay

JOAN: That's exactly why, because we don't know

RYAN: So why are you here, why are you even here if you're just going to sit there and defend it

JOAN: I'm not defending it, I'm just telling you

RYAN: You are defending it!

JOAN: Look, it's dangerous, okay?

We don't know what causes it or who gets it and until we do—

RYAN: They took him out of my arms and wheeled him away

JOAN: It's just protocol

RYAN: And he just was the greatest person in the world and he wanted to be buried, he didn't want to be turned to ash, he wanted to be buried surrounded by grass and flowers this, this isn't what he wanted but they took him away from me, Joan and they wouldn't let me—

JOAN: I know

RYAN: I just wanted to say good bye

> JOAN hugs him.
>
> It's an awkward, sloppy sideways hug since it's in a car and life's not perfect and all.
>
> After a moment:

Why aren't you scared

JOAN: I'm too stupid to be scared.

RYAN: Good, we need more stupid people.

> They pass a smile back and forth.
>
> JOAN puts the car into gear.
>
> Stops, puts it back in park.

JOAN: You can bury him.

If you'd like.

RYAN: Where

JOAN: I have land.

RYAN: You have land like, what, you're a pioneer?

JOAN: My house, it's on a couple of acres.

I've actually got more land than I do house so.

JOAN (CONT'D): I don't know, always thought I'd add an extension or
something, to the house? But we don't need it, me and Lisa, it's a good
enough size for us. That was always what Jack wanted, always talking about
we need an extension, we need more house, I never understood why. I grew
up in that house, it houses all my memories, I never wanted to change it.
Glad I didn't. He wanted to take the house from me, you know, thought he
was owed it since we were married and all, but I kept it because the land is
full of my blood and tears and because my mother left it to me and that
shit's more binding than blood.

You can bury him, bury his ashes.

You can come by, pick a spot.

Get a tombstone.

Plant some flowers.

Whatever you'd like.

> *Beat.*

Only if you want.

> *She puts the car into drive.*

RYAN: Can I dig his grave?

> *JOAN nods.*

JOAN: Okay.

> *End scene.*

SCENE 16

DECEMBER, 1982

Outside of JOAN's home, her property.

A freshly dug grave.

RYAN stands besides her.

JOHN stands besides him.

After a moment:

JOAN: Always meant to landscape.

JOHN: You don't need it.

It's really nice.

JOAN: There are flowers that bloom, right over there?

They're dormant now, but they bloom in spring so he'll be surrounded.

And you can come by whenever.

Always. Whenever.

And.

I.

Brought out the boombox in case you wanted to play something or.

I can sing!

Or.

                    Beat.

JOAN: I can go if—

RYAN: No.

Don't go.

Stay.

JOAN: Okay.

                    She stands next to them.

                    RYAN breathes deep.

                    Puts the box into the ground.

                    After a moment:

RYAN: I guess we.

Cover him now?

JOHN: Are you sure you don't want to say something?

RYAN: I know.

RYAN (CONT'D): I should.

But I.

I don't know what to say because.

He was too young for this.

And

I don't know what else to say.

> *Silence.*
>
> *JOAN is at a loss for what to say.*
>
> *JOHN grabs RYAN's hand.*

JOHN: I'll say something.

But I can't promise it won't suck.

So.

Okay.

Okay, so.

Greg was.

He was great.

I met him through you, Ryan, and I was prepared to not like him. I was. Because I liked you so much, I thought nobody could possibly live up to my expectations for you. And, to be fair, you had gone through a revolving door of guys and I could never picture that door stopping its spinning, but I could as soon as I met Greg.

The two of you fit so perfectly together.

Even if he was never going to finish that deck.

He just had the kindest eyes.

And the gentlest soul.

And he was for you, Ryan.

He was for you.

I think the saddest thing about him getting sick was that he couldn't dance anymore.

Because Greg was a dancer.

> *GREG appears in a spotlight, healthy and alive.*
>
> *He strikes a pose.*

RYAN: He.

> *He can't go on.*

GREG begins to do a dance, a solo dance. It's upbeat and fun.

RYAN picks up a handful of dirt.

While he does, he notices GREG.

Throws it onto the grave.

While JOHN and JOAN throw their handfuls of dirt onto the grave, RYAN begins to dance with GREG.

Lights go out on JOHN and JOAN, and RYAN and GREG dance in their own little world.

They're scored by some music when he joins him.

They dance together.

They dance and dance together until

The lights go out and blackout.

END ACT I

ACT II

PROLOGUE

DECEMBER, 1982

FATHER JEROME is giving another rousing homily!

FATHER JEROME: God gave us rules. He gave us the rules on how to live.

Now, what's the difference between a rule and a guideline.

Can anyone tell me.

All right, who here plays Monopoly, show of hands.

Great game, right? So, say you're sitting down to play your favorite game, mom's got the Chex Mix ready, everyone's sitting down to play a rousing rendition of Monopoly and what's the first thing you do?

Besides choose a banker, Mr. Ellis, what do you do?

That's right, you take out the rulebook! And you look at the rules. And what do we know about these rules, you wouldn't just change them, would you, you wouldn't just take them and say, "You know what, I think that I deserve $400 when I pass Go instead of 200,"

You might feel like you deserve $400 but does that mean you should get $400?

Or should you follow the rules?

A rule is non-negotiable, it is what it is. A guideline is a suggestion.

Let me say that again for all of you:

A RULE. Is NON-negotiable.

A guideline. Is a suggestion.

We live by our rules, not our guidelines. Rules are like diamond; we cannot just bend them, can't just mold them to fit our lives.

That's not how this works.

Now I know, I know what's happening out in the world right now,

Divorce rates are rising. Because it's easier to leave than it is to stay. But you make a vow in marriage. You enter into a covenant— who knows what that word means?

Why are none of you paying attention in school, this is an easy vocabulary 101 word, second graders should know this word it's—

What's that, Ms. Richies?

FATHER JEROME (CONT'D): That's right, it's a promise.

If you go down to the City Hall and you and your spouse, you both sign a piece of paper in front of a judge, that's a contract. That's how a lot of people get married and it's legal, it's fine, there's nothing wrong with it except for the fact it really means nothing.

When you enter into that sacrament of marriage, you are making a promise not only to your spouse but to God that you will never break it.

And if you do?

That's a sin.

You've got to follow God's rules; however difficult they may seem.

Let us reflect on this during our Advent season, as we ready ourselves for the birth of our Lord.

Lights go off on him as they rise again on...

SCENE 1

DECEMBER, 1982

JOHN enters his home.

CHARLES is sitting on the couch.

More dots freckle his skin.

CHARLES: How was it?

JOHN: Good.

Cold.

CHARLES: Yeah?

JOHN: Yeah.

Getting really cold out there.

CHARLES: Oh.

JOHN: Yeah.

Gonna be a cold new year.

CHARLES: Did you tell Ryan—

JOHN: Of course.

Said he'll be over.

At some point.

CHARLES: Great.

JOHN: Yeah.

The property's nice. She has a lot of it, Joan.

CHARLES: Is that where you'll bury me?

JOHN: I don't—

I hadn't thought—

CHARLES: Because that sounds nice.

To be buried somewhere.

Somewhere you'll know where to find me.

I don't want to get lost

JOHN: I wouldn't lose you

Silence between the two of them.

JOHN holds CHARLES.

They're silent for a bit.

Trying to capture time in their hands.

CHARLES: Why don't you paint anymore

JOHN: I have nothing to paint.

CHARLES: I miss it.

JOHN: Thought you said you didn't get it.

CHARLES: I don't.

But.

I always liked it.

I think.

If we grew old together,

I'd watch you while you paint.

I think.

I'd sit in an armchair and watch you stare and frown and reach inside your brain and splatter it onto the canvas. And sometimes you'd look up and say something to me like, "How much was the electric bill this month again?" or, "Oh, don't forget, we need to set the VCR to tape Dallas"

JOHN: We'd have a VCR?

CHARLES: Yeah, we'd have a VCR and a house and a dog and

a bunch of other stuff.

JOHN: That would be nice.

CHARLES: Yeah.

It would be.

> *Beat.*

I'm just going to miss you.

So much.

> *Beat. They hold hands.*

JOHN: Wait a minute

CHARLES: Where are you going

JOHN: Just gonna get something—

> *He gets his paints, gets them ready.*

I'm going to paint you.

CHARLES: I look like shit

JOHN: That's okay.

> *Starts to paint CHARLES.*

> *Like, on his skin, in between the lesions.*

CHARLES: What are you doing?

JOHN: I'm painting you

CHARLES: You're crazy

JOHN: So?

> *CHARLES picks up a paintbrush, too.*
>
> *Dips it in paint.*
>
> *Begins painting JOHN.*
>
> *They paint one another.*
>
> *They start to giggle, to laugh.*

You're so beautiful.

> *There's a movement from JOHN and CHARLES being together to John being by himself on the couch.*
>
> *CHARLES moving away should be somewhat stylized, a saying good bye of sorts.*

SCENE 2

DECEMBER, 1982

JOHN is sitting on the couch, looking a little lost.

He stays like that for a moment before JOAN enters.

JOAN: All right, I think that was the last of them, unless someone's hiding under the couch

JOHN: Tom's still here.

JOAN: Still?

JOHN: He's in the kitchen,

I think he's cleaning,

washing the dishes or something

JOAN: I told him he didn't need to do that.

JOHN: Are you going to stop him?

JOAN: ...I mean if he wants to wash the dishes, I'm not going to stop him.

She sits at the edge of the couch.

There's a little bit of an awkward silence.

JOHN: Thanks for letting us come in here and.

Take over.

JOAN: It's no problem.

It's getting too cold out there.

JOHN: Yeah.

I hate winter.

JOAN: Yeah, me too.

I always thought I'd get used to them but somehow they get harder every year.

JOHN: It's a good thing I don't celebrate Christmas, otherwise I'd be really depressed.

TOM comes out.

TOM: Where do you keep your wood glue?

JOAN: My what glue?

TOM: A couple of your chair legs are loose in there, I can fix'em up with some wood glue.

JOAN: I don't own wood glue.

TOM gives her a skeptical look and goes back into the kitchen.

Another little pause.

JOAN (CONT'D): Your friends are nice.

JOHN: They're all right.

JOAN: I don't know, they seem to really like you

JOHN: They're more Charles' friends, he has a lot of friends.

Had a lot of friends.

Ryan didn't come.

JOAN: I'm sure he had a reason.

JOHN: Sure.

JOAN: A really good reason.

Another pause.

JOHN: Where's your daughter?

JOAN: She's got rehearsal.

Directing the church's nativity scene this year.

JOHN: I used to be in the Nativity scene.

I was a sheep and then a donkey and then a shepherd and then Joseph

JOAN: Wow, big time

JOHN: It made my mom happy, anyway.

I used to get sick a lot, lots of colds and strep throat and stuff like that.

My mom'd always give me butterscotch to take the taste of the medicine away.

I had forgotten about that until I was giving Charles butterscotch in the hospital,

to take the taste away.

> *JOAN does a comforting gesture towards JOHN, holds his hand or something light.*
>
> *TOM walks out; puts his hands on his hips, furrows his brow and sighs.*
>
> *Walks into a different room; the sound of him rummaging around.*

What's he doing

JOAN: I don't know

JOHN: It was nice of him to come.

He and Charles liked each other.

JOAN: Really?

JOHN: Yeah.

Used to stop by, play cards with him.

You didn't know that?

JOAN: No, I didn't.

Beat.

JOHN: Can you just.

Promise me something?

JOAN: Sure, what do you need?

JOHN: Just.

Save a place next to Charles for me.

JOAN nods. The doorbell rings.

JOAN: It's open!

RYAN enters.

JOAN: Ryan!

RYAN: Hi.

It's getting cold out there.

JOAN: I'll get you some coffee.

JOAN goes to get coffee.

A tense moment between the two MEN.

RYAN: I'm sorry I missed it, John I just.

I couldn't.

Not even a week since Greg and—

I should've called or.

I'm sorry.

Can you forgive me?

JOHN: I just miss him.

RYAN: It sucks.

You two deserved to grow old together.

That's a thing you deserved to do.

They embrace.

JOAN comes out with the coffee.

Watches them.

> *TOM comes back in from the other room with a drill and a hammer.*

JOAN: What are you doing?!

TOM: Your cabinet's broken, just gonna fix it up.

JOAN: You don't need to do that!

TOM: It's no problem

JOAN: It's been broken for thirty years, it's fine!

TOM: Things that are broken should get fixed.

JOHN: Is that a motto?

TOM: Oh! It could be!!

> *He goes back into the kitchen; the sound of the drill or hammering, whatever TOM's doing.*

JOAN: All right, I'm going to order a couple of pizzas.

JOHN: You don't have to do that

JOAN: You haven't eaten anything, Ryan just got here, and I'm going to have Tom take a look at the pipes in the basement

RYAN: Black olives for me

JOAN: Ew, really?

RYAN: Yes!

JOHN: Me, too

> *TOM calls from off.*

TOM: Pineapple and ham for me!

JOAN: You're all really weird.

> *She goes off to call for the pizza.*

RYAN: So.

Any plans for New Year's?

> *JOHN shrugs as the lights change and the next scene begins.*

SCENE 3

JANUARY, 1983

The hospital in the lunchroom.

It's New Year's Day!

SHELLEY is sitting alone.

JOAN walks over to join her.

JOAN: Hey, Happy New Year!

Haven't seen you since last year.

JOAN laughs.

SHELLEY politely smiles.

Keeps on eating.

JOAN: That used to be my grandfather's favorite joke.

We'd always go over to my grandparent's house for breakfast on New Year's Day and he'd be there with my grandma and he'd say, "Boy, I'm starving, I haven't eaten since last year!"

And I'd say, "I haven't showered since last year! because I'd have showered the night before."

She laughs; Shelley doesn't.

So.

Happy 1983.

SHELLEY: Thanks.

Beat.

JOAN: Make any resolutions?

Lisa said she'd start flossing and I said That was news to me, that she *wasn't* flossing and I don't really understand how that could be a resolution, it's just good hygiene, sometimes I think I'm raising a monster.

I thought about making a resolution but.

Too much work.

SHELLEY: Yes, you've already been busy.

JOAN: Well.

It's been busy around here.

Lately.

SHELLEY: Sure.

She nods.

Beat while they eat

Beat eat.

JOAN: So.

No resolutions for you, either?

SHELLEY: Nope.

JOAN: What about the boys?

SHELLEY shrugs

JOAN: Are you going to talk to me?

SHELLEY: We are talking.

JOAN: Shelley.

We haven't really.

Talked in forever.

SHELLEY: I know.

You've been busy.

Like you said.

JOAN: Yeah, sure I've been busy, I'm one of the only nurses on staff seeing GRID patients

SHELLEY: We all are

JOAN: Really, how many have you seen?

Because I've seen fifty today.

SHELLEY: Well, it's not a contest.

And there are other patients in this hospital, it doesn't just revolve around that disease no matter what the news seems to think.

Somebody's got to take care of them, too.

JOAN: Sure—

SHELLEY: Just doing my job.

SHELLEY starts to get up, JOAN grabs her elbow.

JOAN: Come on, Shelley.

I miss you.

SHELLEY: Really?

Because you haven't called me in months.

Haven't returned a phone call, you've been too busy to go out, to catch up—

Didn't even bother to RSVP to my New Year's Eve party

JOAN: I couldn't make it

SHELLEY: You could have at least RSVP'ed.

It's just the decent thing to do.

JOAN: Okay, I'm sorry I didn't RSVP to your party, I couldn't make it—

SHELLEY: Really, what were you so busy doing on New Year's Eve?

JOAN: I fell asleep on the couch, I didn't even stay up to watch the New Year come in, I was asleep by ten! Lisa and I were watching Casablanca and I fell asleep, only woke up because she started throwing popcorn at me, didn't want me to fall asleep on the couch, I'm tired!

The last few months have just.

Been a lot.

It's been a lot, Shelley.

I mean, God, it's not like there's a time limit on our friendship, yeah, it's been a busy couple of months and? So what?

Tell me how you're doing.

SHELLEY: I'm doing great.

And I'm just as busy.

So if you'll excuse me.

> *She gets up to leave.*

JOAN: We can talk about it—

SHELLEY: It looks like you have new friends to talk to.

> *She starts to leave again.*

JOAN: What is it, too many people talking about me?

What are they saying, go ahead, tell me.

SHELLEY: I stood by you when you got your divorce because I believed that was the right thing to do.

It was the right thing.

No man should ever do what he did to you.

I stood by you.

I made sure you were okay.

But this?

What you're doing?

I'm not interested.

I'm not interested in getting involved.

SHELLEY (CONT'D): I do my job, I put my life at risk everyday and it's not fair and I shouldn't have to, but I do.

Same as you.

I do my job.

What you're doing— I don't know what it is but it's not right.

It's wrong.

It's just wrong.

> *She leaves.*
>
> *JOAN is alone.*

SCENE 4

JANUARY 1983

New Year's Day.

JOHN is alone in his apartment.

He picks up a paintbrush.

Puts it down.

Takes out a phone book.

Rifles through it.

Finds a page.

He picks up the phone. Dials.

JOHN: Hello?

Is... is Penny there?

Sure, can you tell her.

It's John?

Please?

Thank you.

> *Waits.*
>
> *Someone hangs up the phone on the other line.*

Mom?

Hello?

Hello?

> *He hangs up the phone.*
>
> *Looks at the back of his hand.*
>
> *He's got a spot.*
>
> *Picks up the phone again.*
>
> *Dials.*

Hey Joan?

Hey. It's John.

I.

Um, are you busy?

> *Lights go down.*

SCENE 5

JANUARY, 1983

JOAN is digging a grave. There are a few more tombstones than there were.

LISA comes to her.

She watches her for a moment.

LISA: Mom.

People are starting to talk.

JOAN: Oh yeah?

What are they saying.

LISA: Guess.

JOAN: I don't need to guess, I know.

LISA: So?

JOAN: So let them talk.

They've been talking since the divorce, let them talk about this.

LISA: What about Uncle Jerome?

JOAN: What about him

LISA: He keeps trying to call—

JOAN: I know, I am well aware of what Jerome is saying

LISA: He's like.

Talking about it at church, though.

JOAN: That's unsurprising.

LISA: I mean like.

He doesn't mention any names but.

Everyone knows he's talking about us and

JOAN: Is Father Jerome God?

LISA: No, but—

JOAN: Then I don't really care what he has to say.

LISA: But he's like a harbinger of God

JOAN: That's— you're not using that word right

LISA: Or God speaks through him or something I dunno!

JOAN: Well. I haven't been struck down yet.

LISA: Why do you have to be like this?

JOAN: I'm not being like anything

LISA: Yes, you are, you always have to do this

JOAN: Do what, what am I doing?

LISA: Whatever you want!

You just do whatever you want and make people talk about you, like you went and got the divorce, and now you're digging graves for dead queers, I don't understand why you have to go and like do everything the opposite of what we're supposed to do!

JOAN: Says the woman who wants to be a police officer

LISA: Lots of women are police officers

JOAN: It's a man's job

LISA: You're such a hypocrite, mom!

JOAN: Newsflash, Lisa, everybody in the entire world is a hypocrite!

LISA: You can't just say being a police officer is a man's job and then act like it's okay doing what you're doing, it doesn't work that way.

JOAN: Then how does it work, Lisa?

You're such an adult, please, enlighten me.

I would love to hear how this world is supposed to work because yes, I shouldn't have to turn our backyard into a cemetery for dead men but that's what I'm stuck doing because there's nothing else I can do. You tell me how you're able to look in the face of a kid who's dying, who's crying for his mother and how I'm supposed to give a shit about what God does or doesn't want.

You explain to me how that's okay.

You explain to me how I was supposed to stay with your father.

Do you see my hand?

You see how I can barely close it,

that's because of him.

LISA: No

JOAN: He did that to me because I burned his dinner.

You weren't there.

I didn't want to tell you but.

What am I supposed to.

And it's not fair that I can barely close it

and it's not fair these men have nowhere to go but our backyard and

why was I supposed to stay with him, because I made a vow?

JOAN (CONT'D): He broke his vow too, Lisa, he shattered it and left me to pick up the pieces

and the pieces are too small for me to put back together so don't you dare tell ME.

How it works.

> *Goes back to digging.*

> *LISA stands for a moment.*

LISA: Mom.

JOAN: What, Lisa?

LISA: Do you need any help?

> *Beat.*

I can help you.

If your hand.

JOAN: Sure.

> *She grabs a shovel. Helps her mom.*

LISA: So.

Who's this for?

JOAN: Do you remember Gerald from the choir?

LISA: Yeah

JOAN: It's him

LISA: Oh.

I didn't even know he was

JOAN: Yeah, he was.

You know Chuckie, the tenor?

LISA: Yeah

JOAN: They were together.

LISA: Shit.

I didn't even know he was sick.

JOAN: Yeah, well.

It happens fast.

Chuckie's sick, too.

LISA: Why?

JOAN: No one knows.

LISA: Shit.

JOAN: Yup, shit is right.

They dig for a moment.

While they dig, GERALD appears.

We can hear "Ave Maria" begin to play.

LISA: He used to sing the most beautiful Ave Maria

JOAN: Oh, that's right.

LISA: He sang it for Grandma's mass.

GERALD begins to sing "Ave Maria."

JOAN: That's right.

That's right.

I had forgotten.

It was the most beautiful "Ave Maria."

They stop digging.

GERALD continues to sing "Ave Maria."

It's the most beautiful "Ave Maria."

"Ave Maria" transitions to...

SCENE 6

JANUARY, 1983

It's church again!

FATHER JEROME is giving another homily.

JOAN is sitting in the audience— like, the real audience, where we're sitting, too.

It's going to be dramatic, trust me —

FATHER JEROME: Why does God let terrible things happen?

How many of you have ever asked this question?

Show of hands—

It's all right, you don't have to be shy. Mrs. Jackson you're telling me you've never— that's what I thought, come on, I have. Hands up!

He puts his hand up, too.

We're allowed to doubt. We should have doubt.

God gave us free will, He gives us the chance to choose. We're not forced to choose God, we make the choice to choose God.

God is in that question, He is in that question of why. We're allowed to doubt; doubting is part of the faith, we're allowed to question God, He wants you to question him because in that doubt, in that struggle, we get to choose.

When I became a priest, I thought all my questions would be answered.

I was raised on the streets. That surprises you, right? But it's true. I had a home but I would leave it as soon as it was light out enough to see my hand in front of my face and wouldn't return until it was too dark to see.

A home should be a safe place and mine wasn't.

I would ask God why.

Why do you let these bad things happen?

I became a priest because I was seeking answers. I wanted to understand why these things happened.

I have been a priest for 27 years and for 27 years I have been faced with the same question a thousand times a day.

It's not my job to have those answers. It's not any of our jobs to have those answers.

It is our job to have doubt. And, in spite of that doubt, to continue to choose God, everyday.

Come, now.

Let us pray.

That scene ends.

SCENE 7

FEBRUARY, 1983

The hospital room.

JOHN is lying on the bed.

TOM enters.

He sees JOHN sleeping and quietly tiptoes to the bedside table, but John wakes up.

TOM: Oh, sorry

Didn't mean to wake you

JOHN: What are you doing here?

TOM: I heard you were a patient

JOHN: Yeah.

Just some pneumonia

TOM: Sorry to hear that

JOHN: Yeah.

Hasn't been great.

Awkward pause.

TOM: Here, I brought you this—

He takes out a book.

TOM: A self-help book

JOHN starts to laugh.

JOHN: A self-help book for a dying person?!

TOM: Hey, you still need to improve yourself, right

JOHN keeps laughing.

JOHN: Why do people always want to give dying people stuff?!

Like we have a use for any of it.

TOM starts to chuckle.

TOM: That's so true

But I don't know!

Guess we don't want to come unannounced and empty-handed

JOHN: You could've just brought your mop

TOM: Nah, I'm not working today.

Here as a visitor.

JOHN: Thanks, Tom.

TOM: Hey, no problem.

How's it going?

JOHN: I don't know.

Nothing feels real.

TOM: Sure.

Sure, I get that.

There's a moment of silence between the two of them.

I found the book in this old second-hand shop.

I go there a lot on my days off, I like buying them second hand, I like the fact they've already had a whole other life. It's a nice feeling, like you can feel the other people in their pages. Books are already good company but they're extra special good company when they've already lived a little.

Coffee stains and folded pages, they're all really nice.

I like them a lot.

I tried to find a book on art.

Not for you, that one would be for me.

I don't get art.

When I was in Chicago, visiting my sister, I went to this museum they got out there, some big one

JOHN: You mean the Art Institute

TOM: Sure, that one,

It was huge!

And it was FULL. Of art!

And I didn't understand a damn thing.

How do they choose what goes up in museums?

Who gets to choose that,

I mean, how some things are like the greatest things ever and how some other things are considered to be trash.

Who decides that?

JOHN: The public.

Time.

TOM: But what about things that are special to a person?

But maybe not to the whole general public.

What about the things that aren't remembered in time?

TOM (CONT'D): Why are some things masterpieces and some aren't, huh?

JOHN: Not everything can be a masterpiece

TOM: But maybe everything is a masterpiece.

  As long as it's something that means something to someone.

  Maybe that's what can make it a masterpiece, right?

JOHN: It's a nice thought, Tom.

TOM: Eh.

  I guess I'm not enough of an artist, huh.

  All the more reason to find that book!

  Get myself educated.

JOHN: What's this book on?

TOM: Ways to be happy

> *JOHN laughs louder and harder which makes them all laugh louder and harder.*
>
> *They laugh until they stop.*
>
> *Slowly, but they do.*

JOHN: Thanks.

TOM: Hey, no problem.

> *JOHN opens the book.*

JOHN: Should I do a dramatic reading?

TOM: Sure, why not, I could learn how to be happy

> *TOM perches at the edge of the bed.*
>
> *JOHN opens the book. Clears his throat.*
>
> *Fake reads.*

JOHN: Ways to be happy, number one.

  Don't be dying.

> *He starts laughing again.*
>
> *That scene ends.*

SCENE 8

FEBRUARY, 1983

RYAN's art gallery.

He's looking at the art.

JOAN enters.

JOAN: Hi

RYAN: Hey.

JOAN: Happy Valentine's Day!

I brought you banana bread.

RYAN: Banana bread?

JOAN: Yes.

I don't really bake but I know how to bake this.

RYAN: Could've just brought me chocolates.

Or a steak dinner

JOAN: Too messy.

RYAN: I guess.

                    Beat.

JOAN: How are you doing, Ryan?

RYAN: Not sick if that's what you mean.

JOAN: That's not what I meant

RYAN: No?

JOAN: ...not just that.

How are you.

I haven't seen you in.

A while.

RYAN: I know.

I'm.

Here.

Just.

Passing through.

                    JOAN nods.

                    Takes a look around.

JOAN: So.

This is where you work

RYAN: Yup, this is her.

  The whole she-bang.

  Bought this building when I was twenty-one, not even out of college.

  Everyone said it was a stupid thing to do but.

  Always knew what I wanted to do.

  Filled it with art and bam, now I'm famous.

JOAN: You're famous?

RYAN: Well-known

JOAN: That's great!

RYAN: It's something.

            There's an awkward silence while JOAN looks around.

JOAN: This is an.

  Interesting piece.

RYAN: Yes. It's a Stinnett, have you ever heard of him?

JOAN: I've never heard of anybody, I don't know anything about art

RYAN: Not many people have heard of him. But.

  He was going to take off.

  He's sick now, so.

  Who knows.

            JOAN keeps looking.

JOAN: It's so delicate

RYAN: I know, that's what makes him so unique.

  Everything's about being big and bold, bright colors, bold brushstrokes, there's a kindness to Stinnett's work, a carefully constructed almost effortlessness to his work that I think will appeal to the broader country.

JOAN: Wow

RYAN: What?

JOAN: Now I know what my daughter feels like when I speak nurse to her, I didn't understand any of that.

RYAN: Ah, well, I love art.

  I do still love that.

  Been following the progression of his work for years

  that's what I like to do, find and follow artists and grab them right before they take off

JOAN: Like John

RYAN: John has raw talent but he still has a few years to

>   *Stops. Because they realize he doesn't have a few years.*

JOAN: You heard John—

RYAN: Yes.

 The world feels like it's suffocating me.

JOAN: But you're doing okay, right Ryan

RYAN: I'm traveling down three different paths at the same time.

 One, the daily report of who's got what and whose funeral is when, mourning my friends' deaths before I can even visit them.

 Two, trying to navigate this world without Greg.

 Three, waiting to get sick

 Sometimes I need him so badly I swear I can feel his body wrapped around mine. I wake up in the morning a tangle of sheets and sweat looking for him.

 But he's never going to be here again.

>   *JOAN puts her hand on his arm.*
>
>   *Looks at the painting again.*

JOAN: I do like this piece.

 How much is it.

RYAN: $5,000

JOAN: You can keep it

RYAN: I guess I will.

 I think we're all craving a little bit of kindness nowadays.

JOAN: Yeah, I guess we are.

>   *The lights go down as that scene ends.*

SCENE 9

FEBRUARY, 1983

JOHN is in his hospital room.

JOAN enters.

JOAN: Good morning.

JOHN: Hi.

JOAN: How are you feeling?

JOHN: Like I'm dying.

JOAN: Any other symptoms?

JOHN: Are you trying to be funny?

JOAN: No.

  Kind of.

JOHN: Don't.

  I won't recognize you.

              She does some nurse stuff.

  It was a long night.

JOAN: Winter nights can be like that.

JOHN: Yeah.

  It kinda sucks.

JOAN: I hear there are places in the world where the daylight stays bright even when it's winter.

JOHN: Yeah?

JOAN: Yes

JOHN: Do you think New York is one of those places?

JOAN: Uh, no

  I bet New York is pretty miserable.

JOHN: I wish I could go to New York

JOAN: Well you never know you might

JOHN: Yeah.

  Sure.

              They know it's a lie.

              But it's almost a nice lie.

  Where would you go?

JOAN: If?

JOHN: If you could go anywhere in the world, where would you go?

JOAN: Oh.

    I never really thought of that

JOHN: What, why not?

JOAN: Because.

    I live here.

JOHN: I mean, you know there's a whole world outside of Kalamazoo, right?

JOAN: I forget.

JOHN: Well, I'd go to New York City.

JOAN: Yeah?

JOHN: Yeah.

    I always thought I'd make it there one day.

JOAN: I hear people pee in the streets there.

JOHN: So what?

    That sounds cool, too.

JOAN: Well, I guess it's harder for me.

JOHN: Yeah, I guess that's true.

JOAN: They're talking about discharging you soon.

    Your vitals look good.

JOHN: Good enough to die at home

JOAN: Good enough for now.

    So.

                    A beat.

JOHN: I don't have a place to live anymore.

JOAN: They can't just evict you, John

JOHN: That's not it

JOAN: If you need help covering the rent I'm sure—

JOHN: No it's.

    She came in.

    Picked my life clean.

    Charles' mom.

    She found out that he died. Came in, took everything.

    Took the apartment.

    Because it was in his name.

JOHN (CONT'D): Kicked me out of my own home.

She came in like a ghost, ignored me, only spoke to me through a piece of paper she handed me that told me I had to leave. I'm too tired, Joan. I can't fight anymore.

They hate us so much. I don't have the strength to tell them not to.

JOAN rubs his back.

He starts to cry, she stops.

JOAN: I didn't mean to hurt you—

JOHN: I haven't been touched in months.

JOAN nods.

Keeps on rubbing his back.

She rubs his back.

After a moment.

I used to live with Charles.

We lived together.

I don't know what I'm supposed to do.

And the worst part.

I still want to paint.

I still want to be able to paint

and there's nowhere I can go to do that.

She keeps rubbing his back.

Don't you have other patients.

JOAN: In a minute.

They breathe together.

Are you allergic to cats?

JOHN: What?

JOAN: We have a cat.

Her name's Janice Joplin.

Got her when the dog died.

She's a little bit of a bitch but okay otherwise.

JOHN: Why are you telling me this?

JOAN: You're going to come to live with us.

JOHN: I can't

JOAN: The cat's not that bad.

JOHN: No but—

JOAN: It's really not a problem, I've got a guest room.

And, I don't know if you know this about me, but I am a nurse, I can come in handy.

All right?

Listen, my shift's almost over, and you still need to get discharged, so let me just go home, get the guest room ready, I'll come back here and we'll leave.

Sound good?

She starts to leave.

JOHN: Why would you do this for me?

She stops.

Looks at him.

JOAN: Because.

You're John.

And I'm Joan.

We're a sitcom, remember?

JOHN: Thought you didn't watch TV

JOAN: I tried.

Our sitcom's definitely better than anything that's on TV.

JOHN: Thanks.

JOAN: All right, give me a few hours.

And then.

You'll come home with me.

JOHN: Okay.

That sounds like something I can do.

SCENE 9

FEBRUARY, 1983

JOAN's home. She's readying the guest room.

LISA is freaking out.

LISA: You just invited him to come LIVE WITH US?

JOAN: Yes

LISA: So you're just taking him in

JOAN: Yes

LISA: Like a stray dog

JOAN: No, not at all

He's a human

LISA: Without asking me

JOAN: I don't need to ask you

LISA: You kinda should

JOAN: Well, this is my house and I say I don't need to ask your permission to do anything

LISA: Mom

JOAN: He's just going to stay for a little while.

LISA: Until he dies?

JOAN: Until he figures something out!

LISA: Okay, but I mean, it's one thing to let them be buried in the background but it's another thing to have them live here, don't you think?!

JOAN: Not really

LISA: We could all get sick and die!

JOAN: I don't think we will

LISA: People are dying like left and right!

JOAN: No health care worker has gotten sick from being in contact with the disease, I'd be shocked if it was airborn.

LISA: Mom but

You aren't

You're not a DOCTOR

JOAN throws a pillow down.

JOAN: I know I'm not a goddammed doctor but I'm also no fool and all the evidence is stacked against this being anything that can hurt us

He's got nowhere else to go.

JOAN (CONT'D): All right, Lisa?

You tell me, what's the right thing to do when someone has nowhere to go and we have somewhere to put them, what should I do?

Leave him to suffer or make the bed and let him stay in it?

> *LISA doesn't say anything.*

> *She just starts helping her MOTHER make the bed.*

SCENE 11

MARCH, 1983

SHELLEY is eating lunch alone.

JOAN enters, sits at her own table.

SHELLEY gets up with her unfinished lunch and walks away.

JOAN: Oh come on

        Throws her bag on the table, aggressively eats.

        TOM enters. Sits at his usual spot across the room.

        They both eat in silence for a moment.

TOM: Nice day, huh?

JOAN: It's raining.

TOM: Oh, yeah.

        More silence.

JOAN: But I guess it's better than snow.

TOM: Sure!

  Sure is.

  You know what they say about March!

JOAN: That it comes in like a lion?

TOM: Oh, nothing about rain?

JOAN: No, that's April.

TOM: Okay then, never mind.

        They chew.

  Whatcha got there?

JOAN: Ham and cheese

TOM: Oh, me too!

        Holds up his sandwich.

        This is a very exciting moment.

JOAN: It's a good choice

TOM: You use mustard or mayo?

JOAN: Both

TOM: Get outta here

JOAN: What?

TOM: Me too!

  Yeah, look

> *He gets up, walks to her table, sits down, opens his sandwich to show her the mustard and mayo on his sandwich.*

JOAN: Cool!

TOM: Right?!

> *He takes a bite.*
>
> *They're both sitting, awkwardly eating their sandwiches.*

Hey uh.

So I've been meaning to ask you.

JOAN: What?

TOM: Do you eat?

JOAN: Yeah, I mean.

That's what I'm doing.

TOM: No, I mean.

Uh.

Do you eat burgers?

Because.

There's a diner near here, they have burgers the size of your face.

And really crispy fries.

Yeah, I eat there about once a week.

Usually read one of my books— I read self-help books, I enjoy improving myself?

And I'll eat a burger.

Eat some fries.

Drink a pop.

> *Awkward silence.*

Sometimes I put the fries?

in the burger.

JOAN: Wow.

TOM: Yeah, so if you eat burgers.

I just figure that might be a thing we could do.

Together!

SO.

Okay!

Bye!

He gets up to leave.

JOAN: Yeah, I eat burgers.

Sometimes.

TOM: Cool.

Very long awkward pause.

Do you maybe wanna

JOAN: Okay.

TOM: Okay?

JOAN: Yeah, sure.

Okay.

TOM: Okay!

Cool.

Okay, cool.

They smile at one another.

JOAN: I watch movies, too

TOM: Great!

Me, too.

JOAN: Great.

They keep smiling as the lights go down and the scene ends.

SCENE 12

MARCH, 1983

JOHN is painting. LISA comes up behind him.

LISA: You want Chex Mix?

JOHN: That's okay.

LISA: It's like. Really good, though.

JOHN: I'm sure it's great.

LISA: Mom made it

JOHN: You can't make Chex Mix

LISA: Yes you can, you mix it together

JOHN: All right.

Still don't want any.

LISA shrugs, munches on her Chex Mix.

She watches JOHN paint.

LISA: What is that supposed to be

JOHN: What does it look like?

LISA: Vomit.

JOHN: Huh.

Considers his painting, looking at it critically.

Well.

I don't think it's vomit

LISA: So then what is it?

JOHN: I dunno.

LISA: How can you not know, you're the one making it

JOHN: They're ideas.

This is how ideas look like.

LISA: My ideas don't look like that.

Offers her the paintbrush.

JOHN: Show me.

LISA: What?

JOHN: Show me how your ideas look like.

LISA: Oh.

I mean, I don't think—

I think they look like words actually.

JOHN: So show me

LISA: I mean, I don't really want to

  so

JOHN: Words are drawings, you know

LISA: Yeah but— no, you're not gonna artist me

JOHN: I'm not artist-ing you!

LISA: Yes you are, this is what artists do, they try to get you to like art by like being relatable and shit, like trying to convince people that words are art, I don't like it, I don't get art and that's as simple as that.

JOHN: There's nothing really to get.

  There's no right

LISA: Yeah, okay

JOHN: There isn't!

  I don't know why everybody keeps asking that, like there's some big secret to get, there's nothing to get.

LISA: What are you trying to paint?

JOHN: I don't know.

  I don't even know why I want to keep painting.

  I thought it was something that I could live without but it turns out it's not.

  I thought after Charles died that that would be it. I wouldn't want to paint anything anymore. I thought I wouldn't want to live anymore.

  And a part of me doesn't.

  And most of me still does.

            Silence for a moment.

LISA: I'm going to be a police officer.

JOHN: I know.

LISA: You think I can be?

JOHN: Sure, why not?

LISA: I don't know.

  A lot of people think it's like.

  Crazy.

  Stupid.

  Even though Cagny and Lacey are super cool.

  Like.

LISA (CONT'D): I heard this one guy talking at church? About how that show is good to watch on mute. For like, the ass shots and stuff.

And this woman was like, "It's dangerous to put those kinds of shows on television, it's corrupting the minds of our girls!"

And Mom.

Well, you've met her.

JOHN: Yeah

LISA: You've talked to her

JOHN: She's not that bad.

Maybe she's just scared for you.

LISA: I dunno.

It seems pretty sad.

That people spend most of their lives telling other people what they can't do instead of telling them what they can do.

Or they tell them what they should do instead of what they can do.

Instead of just letting people do what they can and should do.

JOHN: Yeah.

I think that's sad, too.

There's silence for a minute.

LISA: I think I'll move to New York City.

Be a cop there.

JOHN: Sounds good to me.

LISA: Yeah.

Me, too.

A beat.

Your brain must hurt.

If your thoughts look like that.

JOHN: Yeah, it does.

LISA nods.

LISA: I like it better.

The more I look at it?

The more it makes sense

JOHN: Thanks.

LISA: Yeah.

You sure you don't want Chex Mix?

End scene.

SCENE 13

MARCH, 1983

JOAN's backyard.

She's digging another grave.

Flowers are buds around the graves that are there.

Just the start of spring.

FATHER JEROME enters.

He watches her for a moment before speaking.

FATHER JEROME: I used to kill you at hide and seek.

> *She stops.*
>
> *Looks at him.*
>
> *Keeps digging.*

You always found the worst places to hide.

And you were never really hidden, I could always find your shoe hanging off a tree or your hair from behind a bush, you were just never patient.

Always in a rush, even when we played.

JOAN: You shouldn't be here.

FATHER JEROME: You look like a madwoman

JOAN: Then I look like how I feel, that's a good thing.

FATHER JEROME: You haven't answered my calls

JOAN: I know, that's because I don't want to talk to you

FATHER JEROME: I'm worried about you

JOAN: I don't need your worry, not now

FATHER JEROME: You've got to let me worry about you.

You're my little sister

JOAN: I'm an adult.

FATHER JEROME: People you work with, too.

They say.

You haven't been yourself

JOAN: You don't even know what myself looks like

FATHER: Ever since the divorce—

JOAN: I've been busy. At work.

FATHER JEROME: Yes, of course, we've been praying for all of your safety while you combat this terrible disease.

JOAN: You shouldn't be.

You should be praying for them.

The people actually dying from this terrible disease.

FATHER JEROME: We do that, too.

JOAN: I'm sure.

FATHER JEROME: We do

JOAN: What do your prayers sound like?

Redemption for their sinful ways?

Don't you think they're suffering enough without your judgments?

FATHER JEROME: Joan, when was your last confession?

JOAN: It was none of your business ago.

I don't know why you started being so concerned now.

FATHER JEROME: I don't know where this animosity is coming from, Joanie

I'm just trying to help you

> *He tries to touch her in a comforting way but she moves away from him.*

JOAN: I came to you.

And you turned me away

FATHER JEROME: I sent you back to your husband

JOAN: Why

FATHER JEROME: Because

It was the right thing to do!

All you needed was some patience, you've never been patient

JOAN: I spent the night on the street because he wouldn't let me back in the house!

Don't talk to me about patience, don't talk to me about what was right and wrong

FATHER JEROME: You can't just pick and choose what words to live by

JOAN: That's a cute story you're telling at the church.

Your "why I became a priest" origin story.

FATHER JEROME: There's nothing untrue about it

JOAN: Oh, I know.

I know you were "raised by the streets,"

you got to leave everyday

but you seem to forget that it meant your little sister got left behind.

FATHER JEROME: Joan

JOAN: So I don't need your concern.

I haven't needed your concern for 27 years.

The time for that passed.

FATHER JEROME: You can't blame me for that, Joan,

we both did what we had to do to survive it

JOAN: Exactly.

We both did what we had to do to survive.

So how are you going to stand there and tell me that there are rules, that there are these indisputable rules to live by,

I looked up the word "rule," Father, and do you know what I found?

Four definitions.

For one word.

There are four definitions for that one word so how are you able to stand there and tell me what you say is the right way, what you say is the true way when one tiny word can have four huge definitions?

Maybe all of your rules are guidelines

and maybe some of those guidelines are wrong.

And did it ever occur to you?

That I didn't need a spiritual guide.

I needed a brother.

I needed my brother.

Not my brother, the priest,

just my brother.

FATHER JEROME: What did you want me to do, Joan?

I'm a Catholic priest!

JOAN: And a human.

We're all just humans, aren't we?

> *He tries to hug her.*

Don't touch me.

I don't need you to touch me, I don't even need you to love me.

Get out.

This isn't your home anymore.

> *He lingers for a moment before he leaves.*
> *She goes back to taking care of her graveyard.*

SCENE 14

APRIL, 1983

A supermarket. You can tell by supermarket sounds— maybe some smooth jazz kinda ambiance noise, maybe the beeping of items being checked out.

A WOMAN shops. She's putting items into a small cart.

JOHN approaches. He's wearing a cap, tries to cover up the blemishes that freckle his skin but some of them are still visible.

Approaches the WOMAN.

JOHN: Mom.

Mom, Mom please don't leave, please Mom

come on,

MOM.

Okay, you can walk away from me all you want mom but guess what, Mom, that doesn't make you less my mom, Mom, okay, you're still my mom and I know we haven't talked one on one in years— in fucking years— but I've been talking to you this whole time, Mom, I've talked to you about everything, everything from the brand of oatmeal I should buy to how to mix the right colors to get the exact blue of the sky and I've said I think this could use a little more brown, what do you think, Mom

> *JOAN enters.*

and I've said Mom, I'm in love, Mom with the most wonderful guy and I've said Mom, he left me, he left me all alone and I didn't know hearts actually could break, how do I fix it and I've said Mom I'm sick and I don't know what to do because I'm going to die and I've never done that before so I'm scared and

I just want you with me.

I've said that to you a million times, could you hear me?

And I still make sandwiches the way you taught me how.

And I still carry you with me even though you hate me

and I've never actually believed you hate me

and I love you so much, Mom

and please don't leave me?

JOAN: John

John

What are you doing

JOHN: My mother doesn't want me.

JOAN: I want you.

> *JOAN holds JOHN in her arms in the middle of the supermarket.*
>
> *She holds onto him so hard.*
>
> *She breaks away.*

Come on.

Let's go home.

> *She begins to lead him away.*
>
> *They walk away together, hand-in-hand.*

SCENE 15

APRIL, 1983

RYAN's gallery.

An unmasking of John's latest work.

JOHN is weak but doing okay.

RYAN, LISA, and TOM are all there.

All of them are there. John's artwork is out, all over the place, covered by cloth.

JOAN takes the stage.

JOAN: Thank you, everyone, for being here, tonight,

When I first met John, I knew right away he was an artist

He had a sense about him, an "I don't play by the rules and don't care who gets in my way!" about him, which I associate with artists.

And I still don't know much about art,

But I know what I like.

And I don't like your work, John.

JOHN: Thanks.

JOAN: No,

I love it.

I love your work.

I think it's beautiful, but in an ugly way.

TOM: That's true, that's very true

JOAN: And it's surprising and real and truthful and honest and raw.

And we don't need to understand it, do we?

So thank you, John, for giving us the gift of your art.

When Ryan told me he was planning on doing a show of John's work I said,

"Good, what took you so long?"

I'm glad he finally wised up to what we had all been seeing all along.

And without further ado—

> *LISA pulls off a bunch of the coverings, as does JOAN.*
>
> *JOHN is surrounded by his art.*
>
> *He stands up.*
>
> *Looks at the pieces.*

He's a little overwhelmed; there are more than he realized.

He turns to look at JOAN.

JOHN: Not bad, huh?

JOAN hugs him.

LISA puts on music.

She starts to dance.

TOM joins in— maybe they dance with one another.

JOAN and RYAN join in, more reluctantly, but get into it.

JOHN stays still, looking at his art while they all dance around him.

He walks slowly into the next scene.

SCENE 16

APRIL, 1983

The graveyard.

JOAN sits by a new grave.

It's John's grave.

There are some flowers.

They've bloomed.

LINDA enters.

JOAN is really surprised to see her.

JOAN: Linda?

LINDA: Yes, hi.

I'm sorry, I hope.

I hope it's all right I came by—

I heard that your friend.

> *She gestures to the mound.*
>
> *JOAN nods.*

JOAN: Thank you.

LINDA: I brought banana bread.

JOAN: Oh.

You never called for the recipe—

LINDA: I found one, figured I'd try it anyway.

Did you know you have to wait for the bananas to be rotting to make it?

Well, of course you do, you're the one who made it.

But I thought, "How odd."

To have bread made out of rotting bananas.

And then I thought, "How nice."

That the bananas wouldn't go to waste.

That even though they were rotten,

they weren't going to go to waste.

I thought that was a nice thing.

A really, really nice thing.

> *JOAN nods.*

JOAN: Yeah.

I guess that's a really nice thing.

> *A moment of silence passes between the two of them.*

I'm just.

Not sure.

What I should be doing now.

Without him.

Got so used to him.

LINDA: I guess now you live.

You live until you die.

Just like the rest of us.

JOAN: Yeah.

I guess that's something I can do.

> *They embrace.*
>
> *Time scoots forward.*
>
> *JOAN gets older.*
>
> *Maybe her outfits change.*
>
> *Maybe her hair grays.*
>
> *Maybe it's set to music— music from the 80s and then the 90s until now and RYAN is standing at the podium, finishing up his speech.*
>
> *It's 2017.*
>
> *Let's listen, shall we?*

RYAN: Technology has advanced so much in the last few years, that's it's become easy to forget. To rearrange the reality of what happened into a nightmare that gently moves its way to the back of the mind. Re-told like nothing more than a horror movie to which the end credits have rolled.

It's been diminished to practically nothing and we run the risk of forgetting, which is why we have to choose to remember.

Everyday, remember.

I survived but even I am only going to live so long before I die and then who will remember?

We can't allow the horror to die with those who lived through it. We have to remember.

RYAN (CONT'D): So many of those who died were young artists the world never had a chance to meet. And it's my honor and privilege to present them to all of you today.

This is just the beginning of our remembering.

Lights transition as he steps down from his podium, JOAN and LISA are there to meet him.

LISA is wearing a police uniform because...

SHE'S A COP!!

NYPD, BABY!

LISA: Heyyy congratulations!

JOAN: You were great up there!

RYAN: Well, I didn't throw up

JOAN: No, you didn't

RYAN: Success, right?

JOAN: Yes, a huge success.

She gives him a squeeze, LISA gives him a high five.

You got so many people here.

RYAN: I know.

It's a nice thing to see.

TOM enters, he's older, too, and he's wearing a checkered suit.

TOM: Hey, there you are!

JOAN: I texted you to meet me here—

TOM: I think I had my phone on silent

LISA: It looks like you had it off

TOM: I mean, it was on silent then, right?

LISA rolls her eyes.

JOAN and TOM give each other a peck on the lips, Tom shakes RYAN's hand.

Hey, great job up there, sir!

RYAN: Thank you

TOM: You're very poised, it's very elegant, how do you do that, talk like that in front of people, how do you do it

RYAN: Just imagine the audience naked

JOAN: I dunno, that sounds like it would make me throw up

LISA's police walkie talkie makes a police sound.

LISA: I've got to check in with my partner, I'll be right back

RYAN: Yeah, I need to talk to a couple of people but then we can all grab some pizza

JOAN: Yeah, I mean we didn't come all the way to New York City to not have pizza

RYAN: Get ready to have your mind BLOWN.

I'll see you out there in a few.

                        He leaves with LISA.

TOM: I want to get a selfie with a hot dog vendor

JOAN: All right

                        He starts to leave.

TOM: You all right, Joanie?

JOAN: Yeah, I'll be right there.

Promise.

                        He blows her a kiss and walks off.

                        JOAN walks over to one of the paintings.

                        Stops.

                        Smiles.

Well,

you finally made it to New York, John. Only took you 30 years.

But you're here.

I don't like it.

It's too loud!

You would love it. But I hate it.

It's dirty, too. And it does smells like pee.

My goodness, you would love it.

I can see you here. In the buildings, in the park.

I can see you walking down the street and buying a hot dog from a vendor and sitting on the sidewalk to eat it. And sharing half of it with a bum and asking him about his life

and getting sick of tourist shit so you skip out on the streets that have numbers and get lost in names like Allen and Forsyth and Bowery. Standing on corners, turning names around in your head like poetry.

You were always able to turn the most mundane shit into a masterpiece.

My God. If New York City could have been your canvas.

JOAN (CONT'D): This. This is no masterpiece, no matter what they say.

I won't remember it, not once I leave here.

But you. You were a masterpiece.

You always were.

> *She has a moment alone with the painting.*
>
> *A couple of PEOPLE stop by, take pictures of it.*
>
> *SOMEONE ELSE looks at it.*
>
> *She watches PEOPLE look at the painting.*
>
> *She smiles at the painting.*
>
> *Waves goodbye.*
>
> *Continues on.*
>
> *Lights go out.*

END OF PLAY

STEELE SPRING

STAGE RIGHTS

ABOUT STAGE RIGHTS

Based in Los Angeles and founded in 2000, Stage Rights is one of the foremost independent theatrical publishers in the United States, providing stage performance rights for a wide range of plays and musicals to theater companies, schools, and other producing organizations across the country and internationally. As a licensing agent, Stage Rights is committed to providing each producer the tools they need for financial and artistic success. Stage Rights is dedicated to the future of live theatre, offering special programs that champion new theatrical works.

To view all of our current plays and musicals, visit:

www.stagerights.com